SO-AJB-630

THE EMERGENCE OF QUAKER WRITING

Dissenting Literature in
Seventeenth-Century England

edited by
THOMAS N. CORNS and
DAVID LOEWENSTEIN

PR
120
.Q34E46
sec 6

FRANK CASS

The United Library
Garrett-Evangelical/Seabury-Western Seminaries
Evanston, IL 60201

akh 8040

First published in 1995 in Great Britain by
FRANK CASS AND COMPANY LIMITED
900 Eastern Avenue,
London IG2 7HH, England

and in the United States of America by
FRANK CASS
c/o ISBS
5602 N.E. Hassalo Street, Portland, Oregon 927213-3640

Copyright © 1995 Frank Cass & Co. Ltd

British Library Cataloguing in Publication Data

Emergence of Quaker Writing: Dissenting Literature in Seventeenth-Century England
I. Corns, Thomas N. II. Loewenstein, David
820.992286

ISBN 0-7146-4246-0

Library of Congress Cataloging-in-Publication Data

The emergence of Quaker writing: dissenting literature in
seventeenth-century England / edited by Thomas N. Corns and
David Loewenstein.
  p. cm.
  Includes bibliographical references.
  ISBN 0-7146-4246-0
  1. English literature – Quaker authors – History and criticism.
2. English prose literature – Early modern, 1500–1700 – History and
criticism. 3. Dissenters, Religious – England – History – 17th
century. 4. Tracts – Publishing – England – History – 17th century.
5. Quakers – England – History – 17th century. 6. Dissenters,
Religious, in literature. 7. Quakers in literature. I. Corns, Thomas N.
II. Loewenstein, David.
  PR120.Q34E44   1995   95–21771
  289.6'42'09032–dc20   CIP

This group of studies first appeared in a Special Issue of *Prose Studies*,
Vol.17 No.3 (December 1994), [The Emergence of Quaker Writing:
Dissenting Literature in Seventeenth-Century England].

*All rights reserved. No part of this publication may be reproduced,
stored in a retrieval system, or transmitted in any form, or by any
means, electronic, mechanical, photocopying, recording or otherwise
without the prior permission of Frank Cass and Company Limited.*

Printed in Great Britain by
Antony Rowe Ltd, Chippenham, Wiltshire

Contents

Introduction:
The Emergence of Quaker Writing

THOMAS N. CORNS and DAVID LOEWENSTEIN

"This is the day of thy Visitation, O Nation," announced the charismatic Quaker prophet Edward Burrough in 1654, "wherein the Lord speaks to thee by the mouth of his Servants in word and writing."[1] Among the radical sects which flourished during the tumultuous years of the English Revolution, the early Quakers were particularly aware of the power of the written word to promote their prophetic visions and unorthodox beliefs. From their beginnings in the Interregnum they assumed an intensely activist role and attempted to define themselves as an emerging radical movement through their confrontational writings.[2] Thus during the first years of their movement, as they spread aggressively throughout England, they produced hundreds of tracts which fiercely denounced temporal authorities, attacked orthodox Puritanism and godly ministers, rejected social hierarchies and set forms of worship, promoted the ideology of the Lamb's War, proclaimed the power of the light within, dramatized their persecution and suffering, and alarmed their contemporaries.[3] As Burrough proclaimed, "all the holy men of God Write, and Declare": and so the early Quakers were themselves guided by the divine inner light "to Act, Speak, or Write" as they fueled controversy and challenged the religious orthodoxies and social practices of their age.[4] Impressive folio collections of writings by their prolific prophets and leaders, prefaced by testimonies confirming their authority and exemplary lives, were another self-conscious means by which Quakers called attention to the fundamental role of written discourse in their radical religious culture: thus one testimony concerning Isaac Penington, the prominent Buckinghamshire Quaker, observed that "his Manuscripts left behind, proclaim him a witness against all false Hirelings, and their unrighteous Practices, and deceitful Doctrines."[5] Meanwhile, from the beginning of the Quaker movement detractors expressed dismay at how quickly disputatious and heretical writings by Quakers were proliferating. The sectarian threat was manifesting itself through their dangerous writings: one alarmed critic accused the blasphemous Quaker leaders of having "taken a sinfull liberty of themselves in their printed bookes," adding that "these printed Libels" and their "Manuscripts . . . flye as thick as Moths up and down the Country."[6]

The Emergence of Quaker Writing: Dissenting Literature in Seventeenth-Century England highlights the interaction of the literary, political, and religious dimensions of Quaker writing as it developed in the Interregnum and Restoration. Recent historians of radical religious culture in the English Revolution have rightly emphasized that in this period of intense religious ferment and conflict, religion and politics were inseparable: religion was politicized and radicalism often took a religious form.[7] In this collection of essays, the contributors consider how the radical spirituality and politics of Quakerism were expressed in written discourse and how the substantial volume of writing by Quaker men and women – in the form of unpublished and published letters, polemical tracts, spiritual autobiographies, journals, essays, testimonies, and accounts of "sufferings"[8] – helped to consolidate, shape, and authorize the movement and its culture which rapidly emerged in the Revolution and Restoration. At the same time, this collection suggests the diversity of Quaker writing and sensibilities in the seventeenth century: it addresses the coarseness and colloquialism of George Fox's fiery millenarian tracts from the 1650s as well as the urbanity and learnedness of William Penn's polemically sophisticated Quaker prose from the 1670s and 1680s. Until recently literary historians had devoted only sporadic attention to the development of Quaker writing and its cultural contexts.[9] *The Emergence of Quaker Writing* is the first collection of essays devoted specifically to Quaker writing as a significant cultural and literary phenomenon in seventeenth-century England.

These studies, we hope, will stimulate further work on the intersection of radical religious culture, politics, and writing in the English Revolution and Restoration. During the past fifteen years we have seen newer historical literary studies thoroughly reexamine the relations between politics and symbolic representation in the court culture of Elizabethan and early Stuart England. Too often, however, newer historical critics have neglected to address adequately the crucial interconnections between religion and politics in early modern England; and only recently have literary scholars begun to consider the symbolic and political meanings of radical religious literature of the revolutionary decades of the seventeenth century.[10] The essays in this collection address an important but still neglected dimension of radical separatist literary culture which originated during the 1650s and continued into the Restoration era and beyond. As the largest sect of the English Revolution – and one that produced such an abundant number of writings – the Quakers enable literary scholars to examine the ways radical religious literature actively contributed to the culture of both the Interregnum and Restoration whose social, religious, and political orthodoxies it vigorously questioned. Indeed, more work needs to be done not only on the development and variety of radical religious literary culture in the Revolution, but also on its contributions to nonconformist Restoration culture.[11] By highlighting the writings of this major sect that flourished during the Interregnum and that persevered, despite persecution, during the reign of Charles II, our collection invites scholars to reconsider continuities, and not only differences, between the dissenting literary culture of the Revolution and its rich legacy in the Restoration.[12]

The opening essay by Kate Peters, "Patterns of Quaker Authorship, 1652–1656," focusses on issues of practical organization in the dissemination of Quaker doctrine in the earliest period of the movement. It discloses a level of organizational control and initiative that in part explains the phenomenal impact of the early Quaker missionaries and their writing. David Loewenstein, too, engages the earliest phase of the movement; his concerns, however, are not with Fox's revolutionary pragmatism but with the vivid zeal of his early apocalyptic vision and its verbal expression. Enthusiasm remains the theme in Nigel Smith's "Hidden Things Brought to Light: Enthusiasm and Quaker Discourse," though his primary concern is not with Fox and his followers, but with the rival tradition of James Nayler, and more particularly with the Naylerite Robert Rich, who had accompanied him to the pillory, licking the wounds of the branding iron and proclaiming him the King of the Jews.

The early Quaker movement, rightly, has achieved recent recognition as profoundly emancipating and empowering of its women activists.[13] Three essays are among the first to illuminate the rich diversity of Quaker women's writings. Judith Kegan Gardiner considers Margaret Fell's abiding interest in the conversion of the Jews, pondering it as a fascinating intersection of gender with race and class in the early modern period. Norman T. Burns writes on Mary Springett Penington's account of her own conversion experience, demonstrating its eloquent testimony to the impact of Quakerism on the Seeker consciousness of the mid-century. Elaine Hobby's "Handmaids of the Lord and Mothers in Israel: Early Vindications of Quaker Women's Prophecy" celebrates the power and heroism of Margaret Fell and many others, exploring their reading and preaching strategies, defining their diversity, and asserting the importance of an interpretative approach that retains an appropriate sense of the political specificity of their works.

Other essays primarily address the Quaker movement in the Restoration period. Thomas Corns's account of Fox's *Journal* has much to say about its retrospective quality and the way in which recollection of the 1650s functions in that later period. N.H. Keeble considers ways in which the new idiom of William Penn, rather different from that of Fox or

Nayler, articulates the voice of Quakerism in a changed world. John R. Knott reviews the Quaker record of suffering in the period before the Toleration Act of 1689, and considers the role of Joseph Besse in transforming early accounts of those persecutions into a vivid narrative which secured a continued sense of the heroism of the Quaker movement but nevertheless reassured eighteenth-century Quakers that the worst was over and that their movement had endured. Ann Hughes provides a historian's afterword on a collection of readings primarily, though not exclusively, by literary scholars.

NOTES

1. Edward Burrough, *A Warning from the Lord to the Inhabitants of Underbarrow* (1654), in *The Memorable Works of a Son of Thunder and Consolation: Namely, That True Prophet, and Faithful Servant of God* (London, 1672), 12.
2. For a full account of the role of writing in their early definition as a movement, see Kate Peters, "Patterns of Quaker Authorship, 1652–1656," in this collection of essays.
3. Over 500 pamphlet titles appeared in the years 1653–57 and another 500 in 1658–60: see David Runyon, "Types of Quaker Writings by Year – 1650–1699," in *Early Quaker Writings*, ed. Hugh Barbour and A.O. Roberts (Grand Rapids: Eerdmans, 1973), 568–9; Barry Reay, *The Quakers and the English Revolution* (New York: St. Martin's Press, 1985), 11. Kate Peters, in "Patterns of Quaker Authorship," notes that over a hundred Quaker authors contributed to the publication of about 300 tracts between 1652 and 1656.
4. *A Warning from the Lord*, in *Works*, 16, 17.
5. "Ambrose Rigge's Testimony of the Life and Death of Isaac Penington," prefacing *The Works of the Long-Mournful and Sorely-Distressed Isaac Penington* (London, 1681).
6. [Francis Higginson], *A Brief Relation of the Irreligion of the Northern Quakers* (London, 1653), sigs. av–a2r; see also pp.22–3. Cf. Ephraim Pagitt, *Heresiography, Or a Description of the Heretickes and Sectaries Sprang up in these latter times* (London, 1654), 136–43. For the response of Higginson and other detractors, see also Peters, "Patterns of Quaker Authorship."
7. B. Reay, "Radical Religion in the English Revolution: an Introduction," in *Radical Religion in The English Revolution*, ed. Reay and J. McGregor (Oxford: Oxford University Press, 1984), 3, 15–16; Christopher Hill, Barry Reay, and William Lamont, *The World of the Muggletonians* (London: Temple Smith, 1983), 8; Richard Bauman, *Let Your Words Be Few: Symbolism of Speaking and Silence among Seventeenth-Century Quakers* (Cambridge: Cambridge University Press, 1983), 72
8. The studies which follow do not pretend to touch on all the literary forms which early Quakers deliberately exploited and experimented with: for a recent discussion of the Quaker long poem, see Nigel Smith, "Exporting Enthusiasm: John Perrot and the Quaker Epic," in *Literature and the English Civil War*, ed. Thomas Healy and Jonathan Sawday (Cambridge: Cambridge University Press, 1990), 248–64.
9. See, e.g., Luella M. Wright, *The Literary Life of the Early Friends, 1650–1725* (New York: Columbia University Press, 1932); Jackson I. Cope, "Seventeenth-Century Quaker Style," *PMLA* 71 (1956): 725–54; Nigel Smith, *Perfection Proclaimed: Language and Literature in English Radical Religion, 1640–1660* (Oxford: Clarendon Press, 1989), passim; Hugh Ormsby-Lennon, "From Shibboleth to Apocalypse: Quaker Speechways during the Puritan Revolution," in *Language, Self, and Society: A Social History of Language*, ed. Peter Burke and Roy Porter (Cambridge: Polity Press, 1991); Margaret J.M. Ezell, *Writing Women's Literary History* (Baltimore: Johns Hopkins University Press, 1993), chap. 5 (on writings by

early Quaker women); John R. Knott, *Discourses of Martyrdom in English Literature, 1563–1694* (Cambridge: Cambridge University Press, 1993), chap. 7.

10. See, among other studies, Smith, *Perfection Proclaimed*; Thomas N. Corns, *Uncloistered Virtue: English Political Literature, 1640–1660* (Oxford: Clarendon Press, 1992), esp. chaps. 2, 3, 5, 8; Christopher Hill, *A Nation of Change and Novelty: Radical Politics, Religion, and Literature in Seventeenth-Century England* (London: Routledge, 1990), passim; Elaine Hobby, *Virtue of Necessity: English Women's Writing, 1649-88* (Ann Arbor: University of Michigan Press, 1989), chap. 2; *Pamphlet Wars: Prose in the English Revolution*, ed. James Holstun (London: Frank Cass, 1992); David Loewenstein, "The Kingdom Within: Radical Religious Culture and the Politics of *Paradise Regained*," *Literature and History*, third series, 3, 2 (1994): 63–89.

11. On nonconformist literature in the Restoration, see N.H. Keeble, *The Literary Culture of Nonconformity in Later Seventeenth-Century England* (Leicester: Leicester University Press, 1987); Corns, *Uncloistered Virtue*, chap. 9.

12. For an account of the ongoing Quaker engagement with the temporal world during the Restoration, see Richard L. Greaves, "Shattered Expectations? George Fox, the Quakers, and the Restoration State, 1660-1685," *Albion* 24, 2 (1992): 237–59.

13. See e.g. Phyllis Mack, *Visionary Women: Ecstatic Prophecy in Seventeenth-Century England* (Berkeley: University of California Press, 1992), and Bonnelyn Young Kunze, *Margaret Fell and the Rise of Quakerism* (Stanford: Stanford University Press, 1994).

Patterns of Quaker Authorship, 1652–1656[1]

KATE PETERS

The relationship between Quakers and the written word forms a crucial dynamic for historians of the Quaker movement. That the early Quakers produced such a vast array of written records has in itself afforded them an unrivalled status among the radical religious groups of the 1650s; and their subsequent longevity as the Society of Friends has in turn conferred an even greater authority on the Quakers' early records as a prelude in the developing denominational tradition. This is notably the case in the study of one category of Quaker records: their published writings. The tracts published by Quakers in the 1650s have been presented as "early Quaker writings" which in turn are seen as part of the development of a peculiar "Quaker style."[2] Furthermore, because early published Quaker tracts are easily accessible and identifiable, other areas of scholarship have also attended to the phenomenon of "Quaker" writings. Quaker tracts have recently been used as case studies for broader discussions of radical religious writing; or of the history of women's writing.[3] Richard Bauman made use of Quaker tracts to demonstrate that the study of the ethnography of speaking need not be limited to present-day societies, but could be applied to a study of the importance of speaking and silence among the early Quakers.[4]

Among historians of the Quakers, the abundance of published Quaker writings, and indeed of written records, has not always rested easily with their own analyses of the early Quaker movement. Richard Vann argued that the study of Quaker history is in itself paradoxical because Quaker beliefs "are almost uniquely hostile to history"; and yet the ahistorical Quaker emphasis on immediate personal experience caused the abundance of written spiritual autobiography on which much early Quaker history is based.[5] Hugh Barbour, in his study of early Quaker writings, felt obliged to comment that the Quaker movement "has always been more powerful than its books"; and indeed that before 1700 Quaker writing represented no "canon" but was a jumble of rather anarchic individual outpourings. "All early Quaker writing," Barbour claims rather rashly, "reflected personal involvement in a cosmic struggle."[6]

The identification of Quaker writings with an individual's spiritual experience is a common assumption which pervades most discussion of the early Quaker tracts. Richard Vann wrongly equated early Quaker writing with spiritual autobiography. Phyllis Mack's more subtle account of Quaker women similarly concluded their writings were primarily spiritual outpourings: the only way, Mack suggests, that Quaker women were able to enter into the public sphere of publishing was through an intense spiritual experience which allowed them to transcend boundaries of gender, and to write and prophesy uninhibited.[7]

Yet although it is undoubtedly true that individual religious experiences informed much early Quaker writing, as it informed all aspects of Quaker belief and practice, it is unsatisfactory to suggest that Quakers wrote purely in order to express an intense personal religious experience. One of the problems is that of the categorization of Quaker writing. "Early Quaker writing" is often assumed to cover the first two generations of Quakers, from the 1650s to the end of the seventeenth century. This inevitably includes the autobiographies and testimonies written in the later seventeenth century with the intention of documenting and celebrating the lives of the first Quaker pioneers. The hazards of such retrospective accounts are well rehearsed by political historians of the English Revolution: nevertheless, the proliferation of testimonial writing, with its sometimes explicit intention of modifying early Quaker history, has certainly emphasized the role of religious testimony in Quaker writing.[8] This is even more true when we add the fact that most of the so-called political writings of the early Quaker leaders of the 1650s are often studied in the form of their collected works, often highly selected and edited, and with testimonial accounts written by their colleagues. Thus chronological categorization of Quaker writing tends to conflate periods of Quaker history which more usually are seen as distinct by political or religious historians of the Quaker movement.

A different attempt at the categorization of Quaker writing is provided in the work of Hugh Barbour and David Runyon in the appendix to Barbour and Roberts' *Early Quaker Writings*. In their classification of Quaker writings for each year between 1650 (*sic*) and 1699, Barbour and Runyon identified nineteen different "types" of Quaker writings, ranging from proclamations or prophecy, to autobiographical tracts, religious disputes and accounts of sufferings. Although this may have been a useful exercise, the sheer number of categories is sometimes unnecessarily baffling.[9] More serious than this, however, is the fact that in their categorization, Runyon and Barbour apparently attribute only one category to each work, assuming that each Quaker work could only fulfil one specific religious or literary purpose. Yet what is clear from a study of the first years of Quaker tracts is that many of them served a whole range of purposes, eliding accounts of sufferings with accounts of intense spiritual experience and crushing political denunciation of the English governments and legal system.[10] Rather than categorizing Quaker writing on the basis of a reading of the content of any one particular tract, this paper will argue that a better understanding of the nature of the Quaker writings of the 1650s will be gained if we look at who were the authors, and what were the patterns of their publications.

Between the years 1652 and 1656, a little over one hundred Quaker authors contributed to the publication of about 300 tracts.[11] More than three-quarters of these authors wrote fewer than three works: the bulk of Quaker publishing was undertaken by a handful of men (and two women).[12] Although the proliferation of Quaker publications in the mid-seventeenth century is certainly remarkable, it should be remembered that there were by 1660 an estimated 40,000 Quakers nation-wide; and that they continued to grow in number until the 1680s.[13] Individual religious experience did not move all of them to leave a written record of it. Writing was not an inherent part of being a Quaker.

This paper will argue that any study of the "emergence of Quaker writing" should take into account the historical circumstances which gave rise to the phenomenon of Quaker publishing. The body of Quaker tracts, which are so easily identified as a category for discussion by scholars, are often taken to represent generically the significance and development of Quaker ideas. Little attention is paid to the role which Quaker publications played within the wider movement, and indeed their part in publicizing the incipient movement to the outside world. Patterns of Quaker authorship show that Quaker publications were produced by an effective leadership, intent on consolidating a potentially disparate movement and on establishing a sense of cohesion and unity among its members. That scholars tend to view "Quaker writings" as a straightforward reflection of Quaker ideas is a product of the Quaker movement's own impulse to establish itself as a recognizable phenomenon. Quaker tracts in the 1650s asserted their "Quaker" identity over the identity of the author, proclaiming that they were written "by one in scorn called a Quaker," whose author was known merely "to the world" by his or her proper name. In the later seventeenth and eighteenth centuries, the "Quaker" status of these early tracts was compounded by the decision of an increasingly hierarchical and formalized Quaker church to collect and keep copies of all their publications, and to reissue collected editions of the works by the most prolific of the Quaker authors.[14] This collective status is in contrast to the publications of other religious groups of the 1650s. Baptist publications are more frequently discussed as the work of individual authors.[15] In the recent vituperative debate on the Ranters, where so much rested on the authors of a few published tracts, one point which remained unexplored was the status of those publications within the wider context of the Ranter "milieu."[16] Because of the controversial nature of radical religious writing and printing in the mid-seventeenth century, scholarship focusses very largely on the content and language of the publications. Yet one of most important features which has emerged from recent exchanges between historians, literary scholars and cultural theorists is that establishing the context of historical texts is fundamental to their significance.[17] The unique and fulsome records of their own movement left by the Quakers, in the form of vast collections of manuscript letters, provide ample opportunity to trace the circumstances behind the production of early Quaker publications.[18] This paper will argue that the authors of Quaker tracts were exclusively the "ministers" of the early Quaker movement: men and women with the power to speak, preach, and carry their ideas across the country. Their writing was an integral part of their ministry: as the movement grew in scope and size after 1652, so writing and printing developed as a specific tool of an increasingly mobile and vocal Quaker leadership.

The notion of a "Quaker ministry" runs contrary to many basic conceptions surrounding the early Quaker movement. The Quakers were and are famous for their denunciation of the trained ministers of the Church of England, deriding them as "hireling priests" who made a "trade in other men's words" and relied on their worldly learning to command religious authority. Religious sociologists identify as a constant characteristic of Quakerism that formal ministry has no part to play in its worship.[19] Despite this, it is clear that there was within the early Quaker movement a body of men and women acting as an effective leadership, and who referred to themselves as the "Ministry."[20] Known within the denominational tradition as the First Publishers of Truth, these "ministers" were itinerant preachers, numbering between seventy and 240, who traveled the country and were initially responsible for the spread of Quaker ideas. It is precisely these "ministers" who are best known within the early history of the Quaker movement: figures like George Fox, James Nayler, Edward Burrough and William Dewsbery. In addition to their more famous proselytising, the Quaker ministers also carried out a number of tasks connected with the discipline and organization of the early movement, taking responsibility for the formal "casting out" of the more out-spoken Quaker preachers, disciplining wayward "lay" Quakers, and raising money to support the growing movement. It was also these men and women who oversaw the writing and publication of the vast majority of early Quaker publications. Early Quaker writing was essentially carried out by the early leadership.

In 1974 the ethnographer Richard Bauman identified the "Quaker minister" as enjoying a "particular communicative role," and suggested

that the act of speaking itself defined the early Quaker ministry.[21] Since no
formal structures existed for electing ministers, Bauman argued, it was the
process of public speech at a meeting which signaled that the speaker was
divinely inspired. Although as an ethnographer of speaking Bauman was
concerned with the spoken authority of Quaker ministers, his argument
can be extended to manuscript papers and printed tracts. Indeed the
Quaker leaders themselves elided the differences, so often highlighted by
historians, between their spoken, written or printed declarations: "The
Lord speaks to thee by the mouth of his Servants in word and writing,"
Edward Burrough had warned the nation in a tract published in 1654, and
continued, "I write not as from man, ... but as from the eternal and spiritual
light...":

> for who Speaks, Writes, or Declares, from the light of God ...
> Speaks, Writes, and Declares not as from man, ... but as from God,
> whose light is spiritual, ... and from this light did the Prophets and
> Ministers of God, ... Speak, Write, and Declare, ... and from this light
> ... did all the holy men of God Write, and Declare.[22]

In addition to the fact that Quaker ministers claimed authority on the
grounds of divine inspiration, it is interesting that they specifically linked
their leadership with their ability to communicate. In 1662, Edward
Burrough explicitly linked the Quaker ministry to written and spoken
declaration, in a paper addressed to the London meeting of "men
Friends."[23] In it, Burrough suggested that the local meeting should
maintain local worship and discipline, and oversee provision for the
poorer members. These social tasks were clearly distinguished from the
role of the ministry, which, Burrough argued, consisted in "preaching the
Gospell, in answering Books and Manuscripts put forth against us, and in
Disputes and Conventions with such as opposed the truth."[24] Thus
Bauman's "communicative" act was indeed the defining feature of the
early Quaker ministry, but it was broader and much more purposeful than
simply speaking up at Quaker meetings. Early Quaker publications were
a deliberate and highly self-conscious tool of an established body of
leaders. In order to understand the significance of early Quaker writing,
then, it is essential to understand how it fitted in with the leadership role
of the early Quaker authors.

An interesting forerunner of early published Quaker writing exists in
the extant letters passed between Quaker leaders during the formative
months of the Quaker movement from June 1652. The movement's
genesis involved the linking up of former separated churches, particularly
Seeker groups, across the north of England. George Fox traveled through

Yorkshire and Lancashire over the summer of 1652, and as he traveled he recruited to the Quaker movement preachers from these former "Seeker" groups.[25] From the summer of 1652, these preachers were traveling extensively within the north of England. It is no coincidence that it is from this date that collections of Quaker letters begin. Quaker writing emerged out of an increasingly itinerant and absent leadership. The former gathered communities from which these preachers were drawn must have felt the absence of their spiritual leaders. Bauman's argument that ministerial authority derived from their speaking at meetings would imply that their absence from meetings was accompanied by a corresponding loss of authority. The circulation by itinerant ministers of letters and papers back to their meetings was therefore a crucial statement of authority in their absence. "Thomas Goodale [Goodaire], I charge thee by the lord that thou minde thy growth in him, and be faithful to what is comitted to thee...," wrote Richard Farnworth, not to his own meeting at Balby, south Yorkshire, but to that of James Nayler in Wakefield, some thirty miles to the north. In the same letter he exhorted "James" (Nayler) to "watch over the weake ones, and improve thie talent to thie maisters use in faithfullnes...," and "frends" in general to "meete often togather, and stir up that wich is puer in one another."[26] Exhortations to keep regular meetings, and to remind particular members of their duty to oversee the others, are common. In 1653 the Yorkshire Quaker William Dewsbery had written a manuscript list of "rules," recommending that newly established meetings appoint local figures to oversee regular worship and discipline. This suggests very strongly that the itinerant preachers were intent on setting up a cohesive and regular form of worship wherever they traveled.[27] As Richard Farnworth traveled further afield in Yorkshire, Westmorland, and Lancashire over the summer and autumn of 1652, his letters reflect an increasing personal concern to maintain links with groups he had visited. His letters were sent to Margaret Fell at Swarthmoor Hall, Lancashire, with instructions to circulate copies of them "to frends abrord ... to be red at theire meetings: &c."[28] Such letters, moreover, indicate the scope of the authority of the Quaker minister. In November 1652, Farnworth visited the home of Colonel Gervase Benson, near Sedburgh, in the far north-west of Yorkshire.[29] Early in the following month, back on his home ground in Balby, Richard Farnworth received one of the first consignments of printed books from London, and sent copies to Margaret Fell with instructions to send them "Amonge them ffrends there"; especially Underbarrow, Grayrigge, and one to a Major Bousfield "that Collo: Benson may see it."[30] Farnworth also sent a covering letter, to be copied out by Fell's scribes, and sent to all recipients of the books. Farnworth's covering letter included exhortations to local groups to meet together often, and was to "Aquaint them with our affaires." A private letter for Margaret Fell she was to keep herself; another "halfe sheet" was included especially for Major Bousfield and his wife, and by extension for Colonel Benson.[31] Different letters thus were sent between Quaker ministers, and between ministers and their congregations. Other letters consisted of more private, individual counseling. Shortly after his conversion in May 1653, the Durham Quaker Anthony Pearson requested that George Fox and James Nayler, who, Pearson wrote, "both know my condicon better then my selfe," should be requested "if nether of them bee drawne this way, to helpe mee with their councell by letter."[32]

A scribal service was soon running from Swarthmoor Hall to facilitate the wider dissemination of the Quaker leaders' letters: in November 1652 James Nayler, imprisoned in Appleby gaol, sent a paper to George Fox at Swarthmoor to be copied out and sent "into Furness."[33] A paper written by Margaret Fell had a wider distribution: "wee have Coppied one for the Bottom of Westmerland, and another for Cumberland and sent them away this day, we shall send another for Bishoprick [Durham] as speedily as may be," wrote the chief Quaker scribe, George Taylor, in 1654.[34]

Letters were a means of establishing a sense of unity and cohesion within a rapidly expanding movement. Frequently, greetings were sent between local groups and their absent minister. The imprisonment of Thomas Aldam and other Quaker leaders in York Castle in May 1652 was an early focal-point for such letters. The "Balby friends" sent their greetings to their preacher Thomas Aldam; and asked also to be "remembered" to Margaret Fell and George Fox; Quaker prisoners at York castle sent their greetings to George Fox.[35] Thomas Killam, Mary Aldam, Hannah Castley, Ann Dewsbury, Christopher Roods and Thomas Goodwin – all Quakers from Wakefield and Balby – asked to be remembered to their preacher James Nayler as he traveled with Fox in Westmorland and Lancashire.[36] Letters were exchanged between Thomas Aldam and Margaret Fell, who had never met: "my love doth breath out in the power of my fathers love made manifest in thee," wrote Aldam, "thoughe I never sawe thy face, yet hereing the language of my father proceedinge from thee, & throughe thee...."[37]

That early letters were a means for an increasingly itinerant Quaker ministry to keep in touch with each other, and more importantly with newly gathered Quaker meetings, is an important insight into the development of Quaker writing. It was precisely the early ministerial letters, including news of itinerant ministers, instructions for meeting for worship, and reiterating basic elements of a "Quaker" theology which had already been preached to congregations, which formed the basis of the first printed Quaker tracts.

The first such published tract, entitled *A brief discovery of a three-fold estate of Antichrist*, included at its end a long letter sent from James Nayler in October 1652, from Kellett, Lancashire, to "friends." The main subject of the letter was a victorious description of a confrontation between Fox and Nayler and magistrates at Appleby. The letter included the familiar invective to friends to "meet often together"; and the stirring news that Justice Gervase Benson, Judge Thomas Fell and Colonel William West, all notable figures in the north-west with considerable legal powers, were "much convinced of the truth."[38]

Thereafter, printed letters containing Quaker news became commonplace: Thomas Aldam's account of his trial at York, in a letter to his wife Mary; James Nayler's letter to "severall Friends about *Wakefield*", styling himself "A prisoner at *Appleby* in Westmorland for the Truths sake," and warning his home congregation: "O take heed of looking back, lest you be taken captive, and led back again, and so you come short of redemption."[39]

The pattern of publishing letters back to one's own meeting was repeated in a collection of letters written by itinerant ministers traveling along the Yorkshire coast in the winter of 1653, published as *Severall letters written to the saints most high*, in March 1654. One of the letters written by the Yorkshire minister, William Dewsbery, sternly reminded his readers, "I am with you, though absent in body..."; and he went on to warn them:

> you have not been faithful many of you, in walking with the Lord, since you heard the Gospel of your Salvation; I charge you in the presence of the Lord God Almighty, and by his Power, every one of you examine your Consciences, which will witness with me....[40]

James Nayler was equally authoritative: "dear friends, watch over one another, exhort, reprove, admonish in pure love and meekness of spirit, least you also be tempted, ... I shall be glad to see your faces in the flesh...."[41] Nayler's traveling companion, John Whitehead, wrote from Scarborough with the specific request: "Let this be read when you are met together."[42] Occasionally whole tracts were written to the home towns of absent Quaker ministers. Between 1653 and 1654, the Westmorland preacher Edward Burrough spent most of his time traveling away from his native Underbarrow. The first printed tract of which he was sole author, *A warning to the inhabitants of Underbarrow*, was an address back to them, which specifically bemoaned that he did not have the "freedome ... to declare in word among you," and was moved to "clear my conscience in the presence of God, by declaring to you in writing...."[43]

The first published "Quaker" tracts, then, emerged out of the itinerant ministry of their authors. Like many of the extant manuscript letters, such tracts were clearly aimed at local meetings, intending to consolidate them. The relationship between author and audience was essentially that of preacher and congregation. As the Quaker movement and its core of leading preachers widened in scope geographically, so the preaching ministers asserted their authority through written and printed declaration.

Nevertheless, it is clear that as the movement developed in scope, the act of writing and printing assumed the more obvious function of wider dissemination: "they print at one time, more then they speak at a time" accused the puritan minister of Terling, John Stalham, alarmed at the sheer quantity of Quaker tracts he encountered during a visit to Edinburgh in the spring of 1655.[44] The authority of the Quaker ministers' writing could also be expected to function in lieu of their preaching. In late 1653, when the Barebones Parliament began its fatal debate on the future of tithes, James Nayler and George Fox wrote a piece addressed to the members of Parliament. Yet they wrote it in the north of England: it was carried to the capital and its printing arranged by two other Quaker ministers, Gervase Benson and Anthony Pearson, whose legal and political training made them likelier candidates to attend such a momentous political debate. Nevertheless, the address of Nayler and Fox was expected to stand regardless of whether they delivered it themselves.[45] Quaker printing was also used where oral invective had failed. In the spring of 1654, shortly after their arrival in London for the first time, the Westmorland Quakers Francis Howgill and John Camm gained a private interview with Oliver Cromwell, where they found him apparently intransigent. Howgill then published an account of the interview, in the form of a direct address to Cromwell:

> and when I had delivered what I was commanded, thou questioned it, whether it was the word of the Lord or not, and soughtest by thy reason to put it off; and we have waited some dayes since, but cannot speak to thee, therefore I was moved to write to thee, and clear my conscience, and to leave thee....[46]

After warning Cromwell that he was rebuilding all that had but recently been overthrown, Howgill's tract issued another warning on the Lord's behalf: "Wherefore thus saith the Lord, wilt thou limit me, and set bounds to me, when, and where, and how, and by whom I shall declare myself, and publish my name?"[47] Here, writing and printing were a matter of emphasis; and the political motivations for the publication of a private interview are clear.

The first Quaker tracts therefore emerged out of an increasingly itinerant, dispersed Quaker leadership. Early patterns of authorship reflect this. In 1653, when a total of twenty-seven Quaker titles were published, the number of participating authors was very small, and indeed was dominated by just three men: Richard Farnworth, who wrote or co-authored fourteen tracts; James Nayler, who participated in eight; and George Fox, who featured as author of seven tracts. Some of these were composite works and other leading Quaker preachers wrote parts of them: nevertheless, it is clear that a small corpus of Quakers were responsible for the first major output of "Quaker" ideas.

The tight-knit nature of Quaker authorship is further evident in the organization of the early publishing. Much of the impetus for the printing of tracts came from one man in particular: Thomas Aldam, a wealthy Quaker from Warmsworth, south Yorkshire, who was imprisoned in May 1652 in York Castle for interrupting the church service of his parish minister. Aldam was an early and very keen exponent of the value of print, urging books on George Fox in 1652 which he claimed were "verye servisable for weake frends, & Convinceing the world."[48] In March 1653, Aldam told Margaret Fell that he had prepared "bookes" and "printed letters" to hand out during his trial at the Assize courts; and clearly recommended this as a means of spreading the truth to bystanders.[49] Aldam was responsible for sending some of the first consignments of Quaker writing to London for printing; he also undertook the distribution of books across the north of England, and on occasion paid for the printing himself. He was probably partly responsible, too, for his kinsman Richard Farnworth's high levels of output: five of Farnworth's books in 1653 carried sections by Aldam; it is likely that these were added by Aldam as he organized their printing in London. But Aldam's zeal in recommending the power of the press to other Quaker leaders went further than this. In another letter to Fell, Thomas Aldam described his imprisonment as a literally god-given opportunity to organize Quaker publishing; "As the Lord hath sett mee here," he wrote, "hee hath appointed mee to be faithfull to gett these [books] printed...."[50] Aldam was clear that "there shall bee A greate Service to Confound those great Babilonish prefaces," and he urged Fell to find "meanes Amongst you used to send forth 2 or 3 whoe are made free to followe such a Callinge as to keepe the markets in your County with Bookes ... it is required of you in your place to Carrye this the Testimonie of the Trueth abroade. Make some Contribution Amongst you & let some goe in...."[51]

What is interesting about Aldam's letter is not only his sense that books were a means of spreading "Truth" abroad; but that he saw the writing of such books as a particular task to be carried out by a select few, overseen by himself and Margaret Fell. The domination of early Quaker writing by Farnworth, Nayler, Fox, Dewsbery, Hubberthorne, Howgill and Burrough is a clear indication that they were considered the proper spokesmen of the growing Quaker movement. Financing of Quaker publications was also centralized. In 1654, Margaret Fell instigated the "Kendal Fund," a fund which drew money from local Quaker meetings in Lancashire, Westmorland and Cumberland. Its regular accounts, sent to Margaret Fell for checking, show that money was used to cover the cost of printing and distributing books, as well as financing the itinerant journeys of the Quaker ministers. Book production was therefore part and parcel of itinerant ministry; it was also theoretically controlled, or coordinated insofar as it was financed from a central fund.[52]

The production of Quaker books was also closely overseen by a few Quaker leaders. In December 1653 Aldam welcomed a directive by George Fox which asked for all manuscripts to be sent to him before publication, and in the same year Fox had publicly printed a piece which warned all "Friends":

> write nothing but as you are moved by the Lord, lest there be presumption, rashnesse, hastinesse, or pride and lightnesse in your spirits.... Let none print any but what they can eternally witnesse; here all things will be cleare, and pull down that which is not cleare, and cut downe all that which is filthy, unholy, and unrighteous.[53]

Thus Quaker writing was orchestrated from the beginning by a handful of men and women who fulfilled a number of leadership roles in the growing movement. The purpose served by the writing was both to consolidate the movement internally, and to publicize it to the outside world. It is hardly surprising that the early movement was equated by contemporaries with the authors of the tracts. One of the first serious printed attacks on the new Quaker movement was a dogged reply to more than eight Quaker tracts, interspersed with accounts of personal meetings and debates with leading Quaker figures.[54] Other critics were even more pointed in associating the spread of the Quaker movement with the authors of Quaker tracts:

> The Leaders of your *Sect* have taken a sinful liberty to themselves in their printed bookes, as in *Sauls Errant to Damascus,* Rich. Farnworths *Cal out of all false Worships,* and in another book intitled the *three-fold state of Antichrist,* and in another Pamphlet, called *false Prophets, and false Teachers,* described by the Prisoners at *York* &c. In these printed Libels, and in your Manuscripts that flye as thick as

Moths up and down the Country, the ablest of your party, the Authors
of them, have said, and railed, and censured, and slandered....[55]

Sympathetic observers of the Quakers were also influenced by Quaker
tracts, and by the names of the leaders publicized in them. When two
Quaker itinerant ministers arrived for the first time in Bristol, they were
directed to the house of one Abraham Morris, who, they were told, would
be able to "discerne" them. When they arrived, they were admitted only
after confirming that they knew James Nayler and George Fox.[56] Quaker
tracts, the body of which were by Nayler and Fox, had served to legitimate
the movement and to confirm the authority of its leaders.

Thus the pattern of Quaker authorship is crucial to our understanding
of the emergence of Quaker writing. There were relatively few Quaker
authors; and those who wrote and published tracts were the same figures
who traveled, preached, and established and maintained meetings as the
movement grew in scope. Writing, indeed, was a crucial part of their
authority as leaders; and was instrumental in establishing a known corpus
of ideas and figures associated with the Quaker movement. That Quaker
writing was essentially instrumental to the growth of the movement
becomes even clearer after the summer of 1654, when Quaker ministers
undertook a national "campaign" which spread their ideas across the
country and abroad.

In the summer of 1654, Quaker ministers from the north of England
converged on London. Their journeys took a variety of routes: John
Audland and Thomas Ayrey traveled via the Welsh borders, Bristol and
Plymouth, Richard Hubberthorne, Elizabeth Fletcher and Elizabeth
Leavens via Oxford; Burrough and Howgill may have traveled through
Derbyshire and the East Midlands.[57] By late summer, Quaker ministers
had reached East Anglia and by January 1655 were in Kent and Sussex.[58]
By the end of the year, most counties had been visited by Quaker
ministers.

The number of Quaker publications expanded greatly at the same time.
In 1654, sixty-four Quaker titles were published; 101 in 1655, and ninety-
five in 1656.[59] Books were stockpiled in Kendal and York prior to Quakers
setting off on their journeys, and ministers traveled equipped with a
variety of different books and papers.[60] More books were collected by the
Quaker ministers on their arrival in London from the bookseller Giles
Calvert.[61] Thomas Salthouse, a member of the Swarthmoor household,
received in October 1654 two dozen copies of one title, eighteen copies of
another, and two dozen of yet another. The next month, when a new
consignment arrived from London, he was sent eighteen copies of yet
another title.[62] Shortly after this, Salthouse set off for London and thence

to Plymouth. Salthouse traveled, therefore, with up to eighty-four books and a variety of different titles.

The way in which Quaker ministers carried books into new areas affords insight into how books were used by them to spread their ideas. It is clear that they often oversaw personally the distribution and reading of tracts; and that they handed them out or read them aloud at public events like market days, sermons, and trials.[63] The tracts they carried in with them were often non-specific denunciations of the Church of England and exhortations to the reader to turn to the light of Christ within them. Copies of one such tract by George Fox, entitled *To all that would know the way to the kingdom*, were circulated in London before the arrival of the main body of Quaker ministers in the summer of 1654, as was a broadsheet by Fox entitled *A warning to all in this proud city called London*.[64]

Once an area had been inundated with Quaker ideas and books, however, the writing became more specific to the locality. Quaker ministers, upon their arrival in a new town or area, would preach to congregations, argue with local ministers, and hold meetings in the houses of sympathetic locals. They would probably also distribute their books, or at least read aloud from them. Once their presence attracted the wrath of the local authorities, the itinerant ministers would then publish an account of their confrontation. The Quaker minister James Parnell arrived in Cambridge in July 1654, where he was arrested for pinning up a paper which denounced "corrupt magistrates and heathenish priests." At his trial, the mayor of Cambridge, William Pickering, accused Parnell of having specifically decried the magistrates and ministers of Cambridge. This Parnell hotly denied: the paper, he argued, had been a denunciation of such priests and magistrates "wheresoever they are"; it was the mayor himself who had attached the labels to his own colleagues.[65] This account of James Parnell's trial was published: and it effectively publicized both the Quakers' arguments and their specific experiences in Cambridge – including, now, the actual denunciation of the ministers and magistrates of that town. Quaker writing therefore could move from the general to the specific in what appears to be a calculated process. This pattern, moreover, was repeated across the country. Richard Farnworth, traveling through the Midlands in the autumn of 1654, held a number of meetings with local ministers. These were later published in several different printed tracts, all of which carefully named the ministers concerned, the dates of the meetings, and what had been discussed. Farnworth thus specifically denounced his opponents: Thomas Cockram, minister at Swannington, Leicestershire, "servant to the Lord Protector"; "Priests" Hill and Whetstone of Twycrosse; Thomas Pallard, Baptist preacher from Harleston in Staffordshire. By engaging with what had been said in debate, Farnworth was of course rehearsing major elements of Quaker belief. But he also consolidated the actual event of a major Quaker disputation within a locality by its publication and reference to the specific exchanges and personalities. One hundred copies of each of Farnworth's tracts were sent back to Swannington for local distribution in October 1654:[66] the purpose of them was, according to Farnworth, "to clear the Truth of many aspersions, and false accusations, as in the Reading thou wilt clearly see the differences betwixt Truth and errour, as thou Readest with an understanding."[67] Another tract published "Some mementoes to put in remembrance the people and priest of what they did, that they may be ashamed and repent."[68] It was expected not only that such tracts could be read and discussed by witnesses of the actual dispute, but that they themselves could stimulate further debate: "all people, who sees or hears this read," exhorted Farnworth, "try your Priests by the Scriptures, and their fruits, and you shall finde them to be false Prophets, as this Hill, and Whetstone, and all such are."[69]

This kind of local publication is crucial to an understanding of the purpose of early Quaker writing. Itinerant Quaker ministers were clearly responsible for bringing their ideas to a new locality. That their visits were then consolidated by published accounts of their public debates is confirmed by the massive increase in publication rates after the summer of 1654. Such publications inevitably elided the functions of Quaker sufferings, public prophecy, and religious disputation. They often also included brief accounts of "spiritual autobiography," or Quaker conversion. There are thus clear similarities with the pattern of writing and publication which characterized Quaker ministerial writing in 1652 and 1653. Quaker ministers established through their published writings their presence in a specific locality, often after they had moved on, leaving behind them a group of sympathizers who would at the very least continue to distribute their writings.[70] Despite the sharp increase in Quaker publications after 1654, the same corpus of men – Fox, Nayler, Farnworth, Parnell, Hubberthorne, Dewsbery, Burrough and Howgill – continued between them to write, as sole author, over half of all Quaker tracts.[71] They also contributed to the vast majority of all publications, orchestrating groups of prisoners in local gaols to publish accounts of their trials, or writing prefaces to other works. The hand of the itinerant minister was present in most Quaker writing.

To examine Quaker tracts by "type," or simply as "Quaker writing" misses the crucial point that Quaker writing was not simply a reflection of "personal involvement in a cosmic struggle," as Hugh Barbour would have it, but was an orchestrated and highly purposeful instrument of a powerful Quaker leadership. Quakers wrote as part of their ministry:

through it they established their own authority, and the authority of an increasingly visible and coherent Quaker movement. This could not have been achieved had they written in a purely spiritual, introspective way. Early Quaker writing was a crucial tool of the growing movement, and as such it was highly organized and controlled. Quaker writing should not be seen simply as a reflection of Quaker ideas, but is in its own right a central source for our understanding of how the movement itself grew so rapidly.

NOTES

1. I would like to thank Patrick Collinson, Michael Frearson and Ann Hughes for reading and commenting on earlier drafts of this paper.
2. Hugh Barbour and A.O. Roberts, eds., *Early Quaker Writings 1650–1700* (Grand Rapids, Michigan: Eerdmans, 1973); Jackson I. Cope, "Seventeenth Century Quaker Style," *P.M.L.A.* 71 (1956): 725–54; Luella M. Wright, *The Literary Life of the Early Friends, 1650–1725* (New York: Columbia University Press, 1932) and "Literature and Education in Early Quakerism," *The University of Iowa Humanistic Studies*, 5 (1933): 5–58; Richard Bauman, "Aspects of Quaker Rhetoric," *Quarterly Journal of Speech*, 56 (1970): 67–74.
3. For radical religious writing, see Nigel Smith, *Perfection Proclaimed: Language and Literature in English Radical Religion, 1640-1660* (Oxford: Clarendon, 1989), and Hugh Ormsby-Lennon, "From Shibboleth to Apocalypse: Quaker Speechways during the Puritan Revolution," in P. Burke and R. Porter, eds., *Language, Self and Society: A Social History of Language* (Cambridge: Polity, 1991), 72–112. For the use of Quaker writings as part of a broader discussion of women's writing in the seventeenth century, see Elaine Hobby, *Virtue of Necessity. English Women's Writing 1649–1688* (London: Virago, 1988), and Patricia Crawford, "Women's Printed Writings 1600–1700," in Mary Prior, ed., *Women in English Society 1500–1800* (London: Methuen, 1985).
4. Richard Bauman, *Let Your Words be Few. Symbolism of Speaking and Silence among Seventeenth-century Quakers* (Cambridge: Cambridge University Press, 1983).
5. Richard Vann, *The Social Development of English Quakerism* (Cambridge, Mass.: Harvard University Press, 1969), 1–2.
6. Barbour and Roberts, *Early Quaker Writings*, 13–14.
7. Phyllis Mack, *Visionary Women: Ecstatic Prophecy in Seventeenth-century England* (Berkeley: University of California Press, 1992).
8. See Christopher Hill, *The World Turned Upside Down* (Harmondsworth: Penguin, 1975), 231–4, for a useful caution about the use of George Fox's *Journal* in this respect.
9. Barbour and Roberts, *Early Quaker Writings*, 567–75. The classification system includes "proclamation, prophetic judgement, and other preaching to non-Quakers"; "autobiographical tract"; autobiographical journal"; "doctrinal, or dispute with the Puritans"; "dispute with the Church of England"; "dispute with the Roman Catholics"; "dispute among the Quakers"; "dispute with Baptists and other sects"; "sufferings of Quakers described or tabulated"; "toleration tract, usually combined with appeal for the sufferers"; "exhortation, or appeal to non-Friends about specific moral issues"; "appeal to the political leaders or Parliament"; "ethical testimony, or ethical defense"; "epistle to or by groups of Friends or Meetings"; "letter by individual Friend"; "memoir or testimony to the memory of a deceased Friend," "reprinted or translation, other than collected works"; "scientific, scholarly, or technical tract"; and finally "collected works (often including journal)." The distinctions between some of these classifications are sometimes so obscure as to be almost useless; moreover, there is no methodological guidance given by Barbour and Runyan as to how the classifications were finally ascribed to each work. Given that they paid little attention to the

readership of the Quaker tracts, it is difficult to assess how they could arrive at such narrow distinctions.

10. For a different assessment of the content of early Quaker tracts, see chapter four of my Ph.D. thesis, "Quaker Pamphleteering and the Develoment of the Quaker Movement, 1652–1656," Cambridge University, 1995.

11. Annual rates of publication are as follows. In 1653, twenty-seven extant tracts survive, all of which were first editions. In 1654, sixty-four tracts survive, of which four were second editions; in 1655, there are 101 extant tracts, of which seventeen were second, third or fourth editions; and for 1656 ninety-five tracts survive, of which eighteen are second or further editions. The figures for 1652 are less clear: only two tracts, actually undated, but attributed the date of 1652, are extant. Joseph Smith, the nineteenth-century compiler of the *Descriptive Catalogue of Friends' Books* 2 vols. (London: Joseph Smith, 1867), assigns at least one other tract (no longer extant) to 1652. With regard to the problem of survival rates, it is likely that the Quakers retained an usually high proportion of their early publications, although the correspondence contains a few references to books which clearly have not survived. A fascinating document, unfortunately undated, survives in the Swarthmore correspondence at Friends' House, opening with the instruction "Let thes bookes & papers be gathred up with speed to be sent into an other Country." It is a list of "the olde bookes & papers of ffreinds given forth from 53; to 55 & 56," and lists a total of forty books. All of these can be identified as books which are still extant today, and although it is clearly not a comprehensive list of all Quaker publications from this date, it is a remarkable testimony to the fact that Quakers were intent on keeping track of their books, possibly in this case for security reasons (Swarthmoor Manuscripts 1:383, hereinafter Sw. MSS.). This study is based on a study of 289 extant tracts.

12. Assessing the authorship of Quaker tracts is more complicated than actually identifying a "Quaker" tract. "Quaker" tracts are usually counted as such by virtue of their inclusion in Joseph Smith's *Descriptive Catalogue*: for the purposes of my research, Smith's findings were fleshed out with reference to Donald Wing's *Short Title Catalogue of Books Printed in England, 1641–1700,* 2nd ed., 3 vols. (New York: Index Committee of the Modern Language Association of America, 1972–1988). I also collected a list of names of obviously active Quaker ministers from the correspondence, and checked these in Wing's *STC.* Establishing an accurate profile of authorship was complicated by the fact that a large number of tracts were composite works, co-authored by two or more Quaker ministers. It is therefore difficult to represent numerically the ratio of tracts to author. I decided to differentiate between the "solo" and "composite" works of each author, in order to give a sense of the degree of participation of individual authors. It is clear from this exercise that a few authors stand out as overwhelmingly dominant. They are, in order of productivity, James Nayler: thirty-four "solo," twenty "composite" works; George Fox: thirty-three "solo," sixteen "composite" works; Richard Farnworth: twenty-five "solo," eleven "composite" works; Edward Burrough: nine "solo," nine "composite" works; Francis Howgill: seven "solo," ten "composite" works; James Parnell: fifteen "solo," two "composite" works; William Dewsbery: nine "solo," three "composite" works; and Richard Hubberthorne: seven "solo," five "composite" works. Thus out of a total of ninty-nine authors, the individual works of these eight men alone constitute nearly half (forty-eight per cent) of all Quaker publications between 1652 and 1656. Fifty authors only appeared as participants in composite works. Moreover, the same men appear as the dominant authors in each year between 1652 and 1656: their "authority" in the movement was thus consistent.

13. Barry Reay estimated that there were certainly between 35,000 and 40,000 Quakers nationally by the early 1660s, and possibly as many as 60,000. Reay, *The Quakers and the English Revolution* (London: Temple Smith, 1985), 27. Reay is the only historian to my knowedge who actually tried to estimate the number of Quakers for this early period, before formal meetings were established on a national basis. For the post-Restoration period, see Richard Vann and David Eversley, *Friends in Life and Death: The British and Irish Quakers in the Demographic Transition* (Cambridge: Cambridge University Press, 1992), who asserts that Quaker meetings continued to expand numerically until the 1680s. His findings are sustained by local studies; see, for example, T.A. Davis, "The Quakers in Essex,

1655–1725," unpublished University of Oxford D.Phil. dissertation, 1986.

14. Anna Littleboy, "Devonshire House reference library. With notes on early printers and printing in the Society of Friends," *Journal of the Friends' Historical Society*, 18.1 (1921), 1–16.

15. The recent works on John Bunyan are a good example. See Anne Laurence, W.R. Owens and Stuart Sims, eds., *John Bunyan and his England 1628-88* (London: Hambledon, 1990); the John Bunyan "tercentenary" issue of the *American Baptist Quarterly* 7.4 (1988); and *Bunyan Studies* 1.1 (1988).

16. J.C. Davis, *Fear, Myth and History: The Ranters and the Historians* (Cambridge: Cambridge University Press, 1987). This provoked a huge response, which is comprehensively listed in Davis, "Fear, Myth and Furore: Reappraising the 'Ranters,'" *Past and Present* 129 (1990): 79–103.

17. This is summarized, from the historians' perspective, in the introduction to Kevin Sharpe and Peter Lake, eds., *Culture and Politics in Early Stuart England* (London: Macmillan, 1994), 1–20.

18. All manuscript material cited here is from the voluminous collections housed at Friends' House Library, London, hereinafter referred to as F.H.L.

19. *From Max Weber: Essays in Sociology*, ed. H.H. Gerth and C. Wright Mills (1948; reprinted London: Routledge, 1993), 317.

20. For a fuller discussion of the nature and function of the early Quaker ministers, see Peters, "Quaker Pamphleteering," chapter one.

21. Richard Bauman, "Speaking in the Light: The Role of the Quaker Minister," in Richard Bauman and Joel Sherzer, eds., *Explorations in the Ethnography of Speaking* (Cambridge: Cambridge University Press, 1974), 144.

22. Edward Burrough, *A Warning from the Lord to the Inhabitants of Underbarrow, and so to all the Inhabitants in England* (London, 1654), 25, 37, 36.

23. Edward Burrough, "A Testimony concerning the Beginning of the Worke of the Lord...(1662)," in "Mary Pennington her Book, being Copies of severall Papers of friends, wch she transcribed for her Dear ffather," F.H.L. Temp. MSS. 752.

24. Ibid.

25. The best and unsurpassed account of this is found in W.C. Braithwaite, *The Beginnings of Quakerism* (1912; 2nd ed. Cambridge: Cambridge University Press, 1955). Braithwaite drew his account very largely from the *Journal of George Fox*, a retrospective account compiled in the 1670s and 1680s, and finally published posthumously in 1694.

26. Richard Farnworth to James Nayler, Balby, 6 July 1652, Swarthmoor transcript (hereinafter Sw. Trs.) 2:11.

27. William Dewsbery, "This is the word of the living God to his Church," dated by George Fox "abought 1653," Sw. MSS. 3:19. See also Arnold Lloyd, *Quaker Social History, 1669–1738* (London: Longman, 1950), chapter one.

28. Richard Farnworth to Margaret Fell, Balby, 8 June 1653, Sw. MSS. 3:46.

29. Gervase Benson was a justice of the peace, a former County Commissioner for Westmorland, an alderman and former mayor of Kendal, and a public notary. In addition to this not insubstantial local position, he also became a major Quaker leader in his own right. I would like to thank Dr Colin Phillips for information on Benson's background.

30. Richard Farnworth to Margaret Fell, Balby, 2 December 1652, Sw. MSS. 3:45. The book was probably Thomas Aldam et al., *False Prophets and False Teachers Described* [London, 1652]. We know that copies of this book were circulated in Kendal. It may have been a book by Farnworth; there are references to printed books of his in 1652, although none is extant.

31. Richard Farnworth to Margaret Fell, Balby, 2 December 1652, Sw. MSS. 3:45. The half sheet for Gervase Benson unfortunately does not survive.

32. Anthony Pearson to a "ffrende" [Margaret Fell?], Rampshaw, West Aukland, Co. Durham, 9 May 1653, Sw. MSS. 1:87.

33. James Nayler to George Fox, [November 1652], Sw. MSS. 3:69.

34. George Taylor to Margaret Fell, October 1654, Sw. MSS. 1:211.

35. Thomas Aldam to George Fox, York, July 1652, F.H.L., A.R.Barclay trs. 1:16.

36. Richard Farnworth to James Nayler and George Fox, September 1652, Sw. MSS. 4:229.

37. Thomas Aldam to Margaret Fell, York, 3 April 1653, Sw. MSS. 3:43.
38. Thomas Aldam, Samuel Buttivant, Benjamin Nicholson, John Harwood, and James Nayler, *A brief discovery of a three-fold estate of Antichrist* (London, 1653), 11–13.
39. Thomas Aldam, in Richard Farnworth, *Gods Covenanting with His People* (London, 1653), 48–50; James Nayler, in Richard Farnworth, *A Discovery of Faith* (London, 1653), 14–16.
40. William Dewsbery, James Nayler, John Whitehead, George Fox, *Several letters written to the saints most high* (London, 1654), 3.
41. Ibid., 9.
42. Ibid., 12.
43. Edward Burrough, *A Warning from the Lord to the Inhabitants of Underbarrow, and so to all the Inhabitants in England* (London, 1654), 1.
44. John Stalham, *Contradictions of the Quakers* (Edinburgh, 1655), 25. John Stalham records that he was presented in Edinburgh with a whole bound volume of about thirty Quaker tracts, as well as witnessing public disputations with Quakers and their own meetings. He was right to be alarmed: on his return to Essex, he discovered that Quakers, armed with more tracts, had arrived in his own parish, and he was obliged to publish another tract specifically warning his congregation not to read Quaker tracts without a suitable "puritan" antidote (John Stalham, *The reviler rebuked*, London, 1657).
45. James Nayler, *A lamentacion (by one of England's prophets)* ([London], 1653). Anthony Pearson of Durham was, like Gervase Benson, a justice of the peace, and is referred to by William Braithwaite as a former secretary to the MP Arthur Haselrigge (Braithwaite, *Beginnings of Quakerism*, 112).
46. Francis Howgill, in John Camm and Francis Howgill, *This was the word of the Lord* (London, 1654), sig. A4r.
47. Ibid., sig. A4r–A4v.
48. Thomas Aldam to George Fox, 1652, A.R. Barclay trs. 1:71.
49. Thomas Aldam to Margaret Fell, 1653, Sw. MSS. 3:43.
50. [Thomas Aldam] to Margaret Fell, A.R. Barclay trs. 2:159.
51. Ibid.
52. See chapter two of Peters, "Quaker Pamphleteering," for a more detailed discussion of the Kendal Fund. There was also a similar fund set up in Durham. See Arnold Lloyd, op. cit.
53. Thomas Aldam to George Fox, December 1653, Sw. MSS. 3: 39; George Fox in Richard Farnworth, *A Message from the Lord to all that despise the ordinance of Christ* (London, 1653), 48. For a discussion of early Quaker censorship, see Thomas O'Malley, "The Press and Quakerism, 1653–59," *J.F.H.S.* 54.4 (1979): 169–84.
54. William Cole, Thomas Welde et al., *The perfect pharise under monkish holines* (London, 1654).
55. Francis Higginson, *A brief relation of the northern Quakers* (London, 1653), sig. a2.
56. "The Journal of John Audland, 27 June – 30 September 1654," in "The letters of John Audland 1653," F.H.L. MS. Box P, no. 18, typescript list and index by Craig Horle, 1975, 23–35.
57. This journey is described in Braithwaite, *Beginnings of Quakerism*, 2nd ed., 153–61. It is also dealt with at some length in chapters two and three of Peters, "Quaker Pamphleteering."
58. Braithwaite, *Beginnings of Quakerism*, 2nd ed., 185.
59. See above, n.11.
60. Thomas Aldam sent Fox a variety of books by Farnworth in July 1654, and commented that he had had to send for more from the printer in London because supplies had run out. Thomas Aldam to George Fox, York, July 1654, Sw. MSS. 3:44.
61. This is evident from George Taylor's accounts of the Kendal Fund, which show payments to Calvert.
62. George Taylor to Margaret Fell, Sw. MSS. 1:209; Sw. MSS. 1:207.
63. For a discussion of the distribution of Quaker tracts, see Peters, "Quaker pamphleteering."
64. John Camm and Francis Howgill to George Fox, London, 27 March 1654, A.R. Barclay trs. 2:127, arranged for the printing of these two tracts in March 1654; for the early distribution of *To all that would know the way to the Kingdom* before the arrival to the main Quaker contingent in London in July and August, see Alexander Delamain to Thomas Willan, 27

June 1654, Sw. MSS. 3:93. *A warning to all in this proud city called London* [London, 1654] was dated by the bookseller George Thomason 30 March 1654; the pamphlet *To all that would know the way to the Kingdom* [London, 1654] was dated by Thomason 25 March 1654; he recorded another edition on 27 June 1654.

65. James Parnell, Richard Hubberthorne, Ann Blaykling, *The immediate call to the ministry of the Gospel* (London, 1654), 9.
66. Richard Farnworth to Francis Howgill and Edward Burrough, 17 October [?1654], F.H.L. Portfolio 32, fo. 56.
67. Richard Farnworth, *Truth cleared of scandals* (London, 1654), sig. A2r.
68. Richard Farnworth, *The spiritual man judgeth all things* (London, 1655), sig. D4r (mispaginated 28).
69. Richard Farnworth, *A character whereby the false Christs may be known* (London, 1654), 7.
70. Farnworth identified one Anthony Bickley of Baddesley in Warwickshire as a reliable recipient of his "Midlands" tracts (Portfolio 32, fo. 56). For further discussion of Quaker "safe houses," see Peters, "Quaker pamphleteering," chapter two.
71. See above, n.12.

The War of the Lamb:
George Fox and the Apocalyptic Discourse of Revolutionary Quakerism

DAVID LOEWENSTEIN

During Interregnum England, the Quakers waged war against the world, fighting with the weapons of the Spirit as their prophets "alarum'd the Nation." In the folio collection of his works, *Gospel-Truth Demonstrated* (1706), the posthumous testimonies presented George Fox as a "Valiant Warriour of the Lamb, by whom the Lord wrought wonderful things, who never turned his Back in the Day of his Spiritual Warfare":[1] the allusion is to the Lamb's War from Revelation 17:14 – "These shall make war with the Lamb, and the Lamb shall overcome them" – an apocalyptic text that had great mythic potency during this revolutionary period when Quaker writing and prophecy were emerging.[2] Indeed, the Lamb who battles earthly kings not only fueled a sense of early Quaker persecution, but, as an agent of apocalyptic victory, it inspired the sense of intense human agency interwoven with divine forces which characterizes the fierce Quaker engagement with worldly institutions and Antichristian powers. Both a symbol of meekness and apocalyptic triumph, the Lamb had an ambiguous, provocative resonance in early Quaker writing.[3] My concern here is with its apocalyptic resonance in relation to Fox's verbal and prophetic powers: Fox himself radicalizes the myth of the Lamb's War in his revolutionary writings, giving it new, energized meaning and fresh urgency during the turbulent years of the Interregnum.

The following discussion examines the politics of apocalyptic language and scriptural myth-making in some of Fox's most polemical writings of this revolutionary period when he himself was actively serving as the "Lamb's Officer."[4] It considers how his millenarian texts, which announced that the dreadful day of the Lord was coming, engaged with religious and political authorities as Fox attempted "to be bold . . . in the power of truth" so as to triumph over the world; and how their militant apocalyptic rhetoric promoted the myth of the warfaring Lamb during this crucial period of emergent Quakerism when the sectarian challenge was dominating the printing press.[5] Fox's fiery prophetic texts appeared at a moment in English culture when politics, radical religion, and writing were deeply interconnected.[6] While Fox, like other early Quakers, made the power of the light within (inspired by John 1:9) his supreme spiritual authority and the center of his radical religious ideology, he continuously adopted violent scriptural language and vivid apocalyptic images to conduct his impassioned warfare of the Lamb against false churches, worldly rulers, and the social order.[7] The early Quakers, after all, were by no means quietists or pacifists,[8] and they frequently used their prophetic writings as aggressive verbal weapons during the revolutionary Interregnum years. In their writings and preaching, prophetic language became a sublime weapon of the Spirit in its uncompromising war against the world: the early Quaker visionaries were conducting their holy warfare by verbal means. Richard Baxter, unsympathetic to the Quaker prophets, was alarmed at how these extreme enthusiasts could promote the spirituality of the inner light while "they go up and down preaching with great zeal and violence" and using "reviling words" and "railing language" – those sharp weapons of the tongue.[9] Even an admirer, William Penn, noted that Fox's expression in preaching "might sound uncouth and unfashionable to nice ears," though his message was spiritually deep and emotionally intense.[10] Fox's powerful language in his polemical writings of the 1650s is often coarse, plain, and colloquial; and it is often violently apocalyptic. This essay attempts to examine, more distinctly than commentators on Quaker culture have usually done, the verbal and scriptural texture of Fox's vehement apocalyptic writing during the Interregnum years when he and other Quaker prophets thought that they were living "in the last times."[11] Often highly combative in their prophetic rhetoric, his visionary texts during this period were a potent force in defining the revolutionary language of early Quaker radical spirituality and politics.

Unlike his more famous *Journal*, which often suppresses his violent millenarian language,[12] Fox's early pamphlets use fiery apocalyptic rhetoric and bellicose language as they challenge established beliefs and threaten to subvert the social, religious, and political order. He draws repeatedly upon the fiercest language of prophecy in the Old and New Testaments, employing that violent language and imagery as his own weapons to hew down and hammer away at the powers of the earth. Thus in *To all that would know the Way to the Kingdom* (1654), a text urging readers to turn their minds within and wait upon the Lord and dwell in the light, Fox emphasizes the power of the Word which "cuts asunder" and burns as fire;[13] the coming of Christ and his kingdom will be accompanied by great apocalyptic forces that will unsettle all the religious, social, and political institutions and forms of the present age. Fox's writing conveys in physical terms the terror of that imminent apocalyptic judgment:

before him the Hills shall move and the mountains shall melt, and the rocks cleave . . . great Earth-quakes shall be, the terrible day of the Lord draws neer, the Beast shall be taken, and the false Prophet, into the fire they must go. . . . Now the Lord is coming to sit as Judge, and reign as King. . . . now is the Sword drawn, which glitters and is furbished, the Sword of the Almighty, to hew down *Baals* Priests, corrupt Judges, corrupt Justices, corrupt Lawyers, fruitless trees which cumber the ground.[14]

Evoking a series of catastrophic devastations from Scripture, including the great eschatological earthquakes prophesied in Revelation (see 6:12, 11:13, 16:18; cf. Isa. 2:19), the foundations of hills moved and shaken (as in Ps. 18:7; cf. Rev. 6:14), the cleaving of rocks (Matt. 27:51), the melting of mountains before the powerful and indignant Lord (see e.g. Ps. 97:5, Isa. 34:3, Nahum 1:5, Micah 1:4), Fox presents an avenging force that cannot be withstood.[15] Fox likewise evokes the glittering sword of Ezekiel, an eschatological weapon and instrument of God's wrath ready not only to cut down "fruitless trees" (a reference to Luke 13:6–9), but to smite the mighty ones of this world, including false prophets like those of Baal slaughtered by Elijah (1 Kings 18:40): "it is sharpened to make a sore slaughter; it is furbished that it may glitter" (Ezek. 21:9–10).[16] Fox sees himself as a prophetic agent of the Lord full of the Spirit and illuminated by the light within (as were Jeremiah, Isaiah, Ezekiel, and the apostles),[17] while engaged in a great millenarian conflict against all false prophets, priests, and sorcerers who despise the power of the light. If there is to be a new heaven and a new earth, as Revelation prophesies, there will also be terrible devastations and wars: in Quaker discourse of the Interregnum the gospel of the indwelling light and power of Christ produced a dynamic ideology of spiritual regeneration, yet this involved a vision of violently uprooting all worldly powers. The militant rhetoric of revolutionary Quaker discourse – promoted by Fox himself as one of "the true Prophets of God" who "spoke forth freely" to the earthly powers of his generation – was contributing to that radical apocalyptic process.[18]

Later in the same apocalyptic text, Fox conveys his intense feelings of social justice by appropriating the vigorous language of the prophet James to express his violent hostility towards the powers of the earth and announce their doom:

Oh ye great men, and rich men of the earth! weep and howl, for your misery is coming, who heaps up treasures for the last day, your gold and silver shall eat you up as the rust and the canker; the fire is kindled, the day of the Lord is appearing, a day of howling will be amongst your fat Bulls of *Bashan*, that all the tall Cedars and strong Oaks must be hewen down, and all the loftiness of men must be laid low, then shall the Lord alone be exalted.[19]

Fox uses the same language of apocalyptic prophecy and exhortation, based on James 5:1–3, that the flamboyant Ranter Abiezer Coppe had employed a few years earlier in *A Fiery Flying Roll* (1649) to warn the great ones of the earth of "the dreadfull day of JUDGEMENT" and mighty leveling soon to come.[20] To this Fox adds the unsettling language of Isaiah, as he prophesies the Day of the Lord in which the cedars of Lebanon and the oaks of Bashan shall be brought low (Isa. 2:13; cf. Ps. 29:5), scriptural imagery frequently invoked in revolutionary Quaker discourse to assault the lofty and powerful of the world; and in his scriptural allusion to the "bulls of Bashan" (Ps. 22:12; Ezek. 39:18) he likewise evokes an unrighteous world that shall be destroyed. Prompted by the inward Spirit and light, Fox uses scriptural prophecy and language as devastating verbal weapons in his holy war against worldly agencies and religious forms.

One of the most significant and powerful of his early prophetic tracts is *Newes Coming up out of the North, Sounding towards the South*, printed for the radical bookseller Giles Calvert (who published many Quaker writings) and dated 21 December 1653. This substantial text of forty-six pages exemplifies the militant and millenarian themes of early Quaker prophecy when Quakerism was emerging as a revolutionary force about to spread rapidly from northern England, where it originated, to the south during 1654 and 1655, thereby making the feared movement one of widespread national protest:[21] "The Army is coming up out of the North against you terrible ones," Fox's title page boldly proclaims. His prophetic text is itself "A Blast out of the North" intended to alarm the nation, as it announces the eschatological "trumpet sounding abroad throughout the whole world."[22] The tone and language of Fox's text is often fiercely apocalyptic as he addresses the contemporary generation of Cain and warns all England and the world that the mighty day of the Lord is coming bringing woe and misery (one of the refrains of this text): the dreadful day of vengeance is near at hand when "all your hearts must be ript up and laid naked and open before the mighty God, before him where nothing can be hid."[23] This millenarian tract illustrates the sheer exhortative force of Fox the inspired writer who, in the words of one testimony later honoring him, "shook the sandy Foundations of many, and overthrew the Babylonish Buildings" as he performed "with Dread, Power and Authority, which he was attended with from God, which made the Hearts of many to fear and tremble."[24]

Expecting the imminent coming of the Lord and the destruction of the Antichristian Beast, Fox here highlights the myth of the War of the Lamb in order to give special urgency to his prophecy: "Rejoyce, O all you Prophets and righteous ones, the Beast which made war with the Lamb and the Saints, the Lamb hath gotten the victory, and hath gotten victory over the Beast, and the ten horns which pusheth at him."[25] Fox's eschatological passage alludes directly to Revelation 18:20, while also echoing Revelation 15:2 and 17:14 – scriptural passages announcing the victory of the Lamb and expressing Fox's sense of millenarian expectation.[26] Later in the text, Fox again draws upon the myth of the Lamb's War, having just placed himself in the visionary line of Isaiah, Jeremiah, Ezekiel, and Micah; fusing his prophetic voice with that of the "Lord God of powers," he utters his thundering words against teachers of the world now in England: "be valiant for the Lord, bow not to the deceit: tremble all Nations before the Lord, and before his Army, his Host. Sound the Trumpet, sound an Alarm, call up to the battell, gather together for the destruction, draw the sword . . . hew down all the powers of the earth . . . a day of slaughter is coming to you who have made war against the Lamb and against the Saints."[27] Here the sublime Quaker visionary blends the language of Revelation with the militant language of the prophet Joel ("Blow ye the trumpet in Zion, and sound an alarm in my holy mountain . . . for the day of the Lord cometh," Joel 2:1) and the language of Psalm 114:7, while also evoking a prophetic day of slaughter (as in Jeremiah 12:3). Fox's fiery prophecies, in this and other passages, convey a sense of mighty spiritual forces engaged in a great apocalyptic conflict – one involving a God of all-consuming vengeance, saints guided by the inward light, and the fleshly powers of Antichrist.

Fox's text, moreover, includes provocative political commentary that is colored by powerful apocalyptic language and images. Thus for example in the third section of *Newes Coming up out of the North* the Quaker prophet warns not only the present heads of the nation under the Protectorate but "all who are under the Dominion of the earthly Powers, Nations and Kingdoms every where in all the world." His strident prophetic writing aimed at worldly rulers is a conflation of scriptural texts reinforced by vigorous verbal repetition: "Tremble all before the Lord, O earthly Powers, tremble before the Lord God Almighty; to you the Lord is uttering his thunders, to you the Lord is uttering his voyce, to you the Lord is sounding his trumpet, to you the warning piece is gone out."[28] Here Fox's thundering prophecy has fused such scriptural passages as Psalms 99:1 and 114:7 with Joel 2:1. Fox adopts other potent scriptural images to continue his assault on worldly powers. Having stressed, much like Gerrard Winstanley, that laws and justice will be established inwardly and set in people's hearts, Fox first evokes the great tree of Daniel 4:10–12, which in his *Newes Coming up out of the North* becomes a fruitless tree whose branches are symbolic of the spread of injustice; then he invokes the messianic stone of Daniel 2:34–5, which will dash to pieces the image and kingdom of unjust rulers and justices. Then returning to the theme of nations trembling before the Almighty's power (this time by evoking Ezekiel 26:16 and 32:10), Fox proclaims the Lord's kingdom "whose dominion is a dominion for ever" and fiercely chastises England: "Oh England, England, thou hast forsaken thy visitation, thou hast not minded thy visitation. . . . The god of the world doth blind your eye." His verbal chastisement continues and gains further specificity and immediacy as he warns the Protectorate now in power: "you must be cut down with the same power that cut down the King who reigned over the Nation, in whose family was a Nurse for Papists and for Bishops." God may have given England victories over the Antichristian papists, but Antichristian powers still operate in the land under its newest political regime which has retreated from revolution: "the Beast and the false Prophet is standing still, which held up these [papist] things, and they keep their places: so another Parliament grew, and God hath cut down that. Beware of yourselves, for the Lord will pluck down you."[29]

Fox's political analysis and apocalyptic prophecy resemble Gerrard Winstanley's several years earlier when the Digger prophet was challenging the interconnected clerical, legal, and state powers of the newly formed Republic.[30] As both Fox and Winstanley warn, the powers of the Beast continue to operate in the nation: they were by no means eradicated by the dramatic Revolution of 1648–49, nor were they eradicated during the early years of the Republic when the Rump Parliament was in power. Like Winstanley and other religious radicals who were keenly aware of the disparity between promise and performance during the Republic,[31] Fox highlights the disparity between promise and achievement: "you have promised many fair promises to the Nation, but little you have performed." Drawing upon the language of Habbakuk 2, with its oracles of woe, and challenging worldly powers with a series of "woes" common in early Quaker prophetic discourse, Fox stresses the continuity of the powers of the Beast which shall be destroyed: "Woe, woe is coming upon you all, the same Teachers are standing that were in the time of the King, and the same that were in the time of the Bishops, and many of these are and have been your Counsellers, and the same that held up the Rails, Crosses and Pictures, are standing still." It is as though the tyranny of Laudian policies and the Antichristian church had hardly disappeared in 1640. The difference now is that, in the turbulent and iconoclastic times of Interregnum England, the God of power is pouring forth his Spirit (as prophesied in Joel 2:28) so that "his Sons and his Daughters shall prophesie, and thousands of them do prophesie," though "thousands of them have been mocked, some stoned, prisoned, whipped and beaten."[32] Indeed despite persecution, Fox and the revolutionary Quaker prophets, moved by the inward Spirit and speaking from the inner light, were now poised to proclaim the day of the Lord from the north to the south of England as they dared to warn the Protectorate and other worldly rulers, as well as all "dissembling hypocrites" in this generation of Cain, that the religious and political institutions of Antichrist would soon perish when the Lord Jesus comes "to rule all Nations with a rod of Iron" (as in Rev. 19:15).[33]

In *Newes Coming up out of the North* and his other fiery apocalyptic tracts of the Interregnum, Fox repeatedly represents God as a dreadful and mighty power – shaking and leveling mountains, making "the Earth reele to and fro" and cleaving it "asunder," bringing down low all who are exalted, and throwing down the worldly kingdoms as he prepares to reign within his saints.[34] Fox's Lord is a God of fury, vengeance and overturning: he is "the terrible One," as Fox calls him in *Newes Coming up out of the North*, recalling that the day of the Lord will indeed be "very terrible" (as it is described in the eschatological passages of Joel 2:11 and 2:31): echoing Isaiah 2:19–21, Fox prophesies that he is "coming with his power, to shake terribly the earth; and the glory of the Lord is arising, and all the Idols of gold must be cast out, and all the honours must be cut down and cast out, and the high-places puld down, . . . and the powers of the earth are shaking."[35] In Fox's apocalyptic writings, the awesome "power of God is endless": when he overthrows the Romish church, he overthrows "root and branch" and "overturns all the foundation" of "churches and dominions," and with his "Arm and Power" he "layes down the Mountaines with the Valleys, and layes down the sturdiest Oak."[36] He is a powerful whirlwind gone forth in fury to scatter the ungodly as chaff.[37] He is truly a God of sublime hatred who pours his wrath upon his enemies and the adversaries of righteousness. "Thou art hated of God eternally, hated for ever," writes Fox, expressing through his own vehement prose that fierce divine hatred as he blasts the prophane children of Esau in his generation: as the prophesy of Malachi had proclaimed, against Esau and his heirs "the Lord hath indignation for ever" (1:2–4). Thus they will feel the terrible, burning power of the *odium Dei* and "shalt be a wilderness barren" and burnt up "as stubble" (alluding to Isaiah 47:14 and Malachi 4:1): in his fierce prophecies, Fox envisions that "the Lord Jesus Christ is coming in flames to render vengeance upon all . . . ungodly ones."[38] In "the day of the Lords Wrath," all the ungodly who have not repented will feel "sudden Judgements and Plagues come upon" them.[39] Such, then, is the power and "the wrath of the Lamb" (Rev. 6:16–17). The omnipotent God of *Paradise Lost*, who promises mercy and grace to fallen humans who chose to accept grace (Book 3.131–4), seems mild compared to the God of Fox's fiery revolutionary tracts: rather, Fox's God, in his response of all worldly authorities, false prophets and Antichrists who hate the light, resembles the dreadful Lord of *Samson Agonistes* who brings swift destruction upon the ungodly and idolatrous "Fallen into wrath divine" (line 1683); or in the words of the prophetic Fox (alluding to Rev. 16:1–17), "all the plagues of God are to be poured out upon them, the vials of the wrath of the Almighty."[40] In the day of the Lord's vengeance, such plagues are "to be poured out without mixture" (an echo of Rev. 14:10) on the blind priests of Fox's generation.[41] Fox's wrathful God is a terrifying, unconquerable force who is rising and overturning magistrates and authorities: this ferocious vision no doubt reinforced the sense of Quaker fearlessness and resolve which the prophetic Fox exemplified in his righteous and often bellicose defiance of hostile worldly powers. It reinforced, moreover, the perception that the revolutionary Quaker prophets – those warriors of the Lamb – were themselves terrifying and alarming.

Fox's tract *The Vials of the Wrath of God* (1654)[42] offers another striking example of the kind of revolutionary rhetoric Fox exploited early in his prophetic career when he was at war with the world and proclaiming that the day of the Lord is coming. His prophetic discourse, addressed like the fiery writing of Abiezer Coppe to "Great men, and Rich men," derives its potency by employing both vigorous verbal repetition and a mosaic of scriptural allusions to characterize graphically the wilderness of England in an unrighteous age:

> Tremble and be astonished you heathen that knows not God; for you are all heathens that know not God, and the land is full of crooked waies, the land is full of rough places, the land is full of hills and mountains, the land is full of bryers and thorns, dogs and swine, fighting and barking, snarling and biting one another, for the husks, and for the earthly creatures.[43]

Here Fox has woven together phrases from a variety of scriptural passages including Proverbs 2:15 ("crooked waies"; cf. Lam. 3:9, Ps. 125:5), Isaiah 40:4 and 42:15 (the land "full of rough places" and hills and mountains which shall be laid low), and Isaiah 7:24 (the land full of "bryers and thorns"). Fox's vision of the land full of dogs and swine fighting for the husks evokes Revelation 22:15, which describes those outside the kingdom of God as "dogs, and sorcerers, and whoremongers, and murderers, and idolaters, and whosoever loveth and maketh a lie," an apocalyptic passage Fox cites in *Newes coming up out of the North*;[44] and it seems to recall as well "the husks that the swine did eat" in Luke 15:16. But Fox's powerful image of the dogs and swine fighting, barking, snarling, and biting gives the ungodly of the world a particularly vicious and bestial character.[45] Fox's hostile ungodly world is indeed one of scorners, dissemblers, "quarrellers, fighters, stoners, wrathful malicious ones" and other vicious haters of the light within.[46] Fox relegates them all to the level of subhuman beasts in a vigorous catalogue of epithets: "ye goats, ye wolves, ye dogs, ye swine, ye serpents, ye vulterous ones, ye beasts, ye lyons, ye strong hourses neighing up and down, walking after your lusts." Such fierce "Scripture-language," as Fox calls it in *The Vials of the Wrath of God* (he insists "this is not railing"),[47] contributes to the coarse, raw texture of his highly confrontational writing, augmenting its prophetic authority and violent denunciation of a hostile world.

Scriptural allusions and phrases have an immediate potency for Fox who reinvigorates them as he uses them to combat the ungodly world in its multiple manifestations. Thus, for example, working from the passage in Luke 13:6–9, which concerns the fruitless tree which cumbers the ground, Fox in *The Vials* powerfully exploits the repetition of a key phrase along with its variation as his prophetic writing increases in its emotional vehemence:

> Cumber not the ground ye fruitless trees; ye proud ones, ye scorners, cumber not the ground; ye drunkards, ye cumber the ground; ye cumber the ground, ye lyers, cheaters and cozeners; ye cumber the ground, who use deceit; ye mockers and lustful ones, which devours the creation, ye are the fruitless trees that cumber the ground; you fair outside professors and teachers, you cumber the ground, who lives in high swelling words . . . and you are the trees that bear leaves, but no fruit; so ye are they that cumber the ground.

The scriptural "fruitless trees" become, in Fox's visionary writing, all the many worldly or fleshly powers in his age which "cumber the ground" and which, as Winstanley himself might have put it, "devour the creation."[48] Then piling up epithets and again employing verbal repetition based on the same scriptural text, Fox continues his prophetic assault: "Drunkard, swearer, cursed speaker, thou art this corrupt evil tree, whoremonger, envious one, fighter, quarrellers, malicious ones, scorner, mocker, reproacher, thou art this corrupt tree, that cannot bring forth good fruit. . . ." A page later Fox reiterates and varies his prophecy by inserting a series of "woes": "Woe unto you drunkards; ye cumber the ground; woe unto you hypocrites, ye cumber the ground; woe unto you lyers, ye cumber the ground. . . ." The prophetic Fox, who reviles any form of secular play and festive culture, can likewise convey his stern condemnation through a vigorous list of activities associated with an ungodly and ensnaring world: thus he blasts the lustful ones who follow "pleasure, rioting, feasting, sporting, drunkenness, gluttony, hawking, hunting, *Esau*-like, ye cumber the ground." The symbolic reference to Esau at the end of Fox's list places the whole condemnation in a larger scriptural-historical context: this is the current generation of Esau, as well as Cain, that the prophetic Fox is lambasting. Such passages, with their energetic verbal repetition, convey the coarseness of Fox's visionary prose as well as its undeniable rhetorical power. The frequent use of verbal repetition, a notable feature of Fox's prophetic tracts, underscores a sense of urgency, as well as a sense of impending judgment as Fox envisions his apocalyptic Lord "coming in power to sweep the land of evil doers, and to hew down you fruitless trees which cumber the ground."[49]

Published during the same year, Fox's fiery text, *The Trumpet of the Lord Sounded, And his Sword Drawn* (1654), proclaims that the Lord's apocalyptic sword will now separate "the Precious and the Vile," much as Fox, the spiritual visionary, attempts to discern between the two. The prophecy is issued by those "who have come thorow great tribulation, whose garments have been washed in the blood of the LAMB," a reference to Revelation 7:14 and to Quaker martyrdom and purity in an age full of spiritual dissimulation and Antichristian sorcery.[50] The tract highlights, among its principal themes, the treachery of dissimulation in relation to orthodox religion – one can "make a profession of God and Christ, and make a fair shew to the world, and yet be an hypocrite," especially at a moment when "the well-favoured harlot . . . is painted with the Saints words, and with Christs." Like Abiezer Coppe, Fox makes the Antichristian harlot a symbol of the subtlety of formal, external religion (as opposed to the religion of the Spirit within) engaged in "deceiving the simple, and ensnaring them."[51] Fox depicts the theatricalism of the clerical establishment whose priests have made a trade of the spiritual words of the prophets and apostles: the minister who preaches Christ without is "like a Stage-player, which acts a Stage-play aloft, with Points, and Reasons, . . . and Authors, and old Fathers, and Tryals, and Mattens . . . and where they will not give him money, he will not act his Play there."[52] Resorting to the kind of verbal repetition he often employs so energetically, the prophetic Fox conveys a sense of a world full of deceitful practices and conjuring as he foresees the consequences of the day of the Lord "coming in power": "all secret pride, and secret envie, and secret malice, and secret revenge, and secret subtilty, and secret hypocrisie, and secret dissimulation, shall be laid open, and made manifest."[53] The tract concludes with passages of visionary warning which proclaim woe "to all the Priests of *England*" and announce that the "Lord God of power" is thundering against all "Powers of Witchcraft, Charmers, and Inchanters": "For the day of the Lords wrath is coming among you; a day of Vengeance: the fire is kindling. . . . now is the hand of the Lord of hosts upon you all, and his Army is gathering, and his Sword is drawn, which hath two edges, that before him none should escape." At such moments of violent apocalypticism, the active Quaker visionary blends his voice with that of the militant Lord's. His scorching words and the Word have become one: "The Lord hath spoken it. To you all, this is the word of the Lord."[54]

Later during this revolutionary decade Fox produced two notable apocalyptic works: *The Great Mistery of the Great Whore Unfolded: and Antichrists Kingdom Revealed unto Destruction* (1659), containing a lengthy prefatory epistle by the Quaker prophet Edward Burrough, and *The Lambs Officer* (1659). Drawing extensively upon the myth of the Lamb's War in a powerful account of Quaker spiritual ideology, suffering, and persecution, Burrough proclaims that in fighting their righteous wars of truth with the sword of Revelation ("the sword that goes out of his mouth") "the followers of the Lamb" have become "an Army dreadful and terrible before whom the wicked do fear and tremble," so that "they that follow the Lamb shall overcome."[55] Moreover, in the massive main text of *The Great Mistery*, Fox employs, as he vehemently responds to countless Quaker detractors, the violent language of Revelation; thus he wages his verbal warfare on behalf of the saints and highlights a sense of mighty apocalyptic forces engaged in fierce spiritual conflict at this very moment: "*now* is the vials, and thunders, and plagues, and trumpets sounding and going forth . . . And *now* are the Kings of the Earth, and the Beast, and the false Prophets, and Antichrists . . . gathering together, with the old deceiver the Devil, to battle against the Lamb" (emphasis added). And so while the godly soldiers strengthen themselves with the light within, "all those false Prophets, Beasts, Antichrists, and mother of Harlots, great Whore, and Kings of the Earth, and the Devill, are making War against the *Lamb* and the Saints. . . . Now are all the *Antichrists* appearing, and are in armes, and rising against Christ and his *light*." The dramatic sense of the early Quakers at war with "the whole world . . . standing against the light" was constantly expressed in such bellicose language and fervent apocalyptic images.[56]

Fox's apocalyptic fervor and rhetorical power as a prophetic writer are particularly evident in *The Lambs Officer*, the last visionary text I want to consider here. This forceful apocalyptic text appeared during 1659, a year of radical exhilaration during which occurred a wave of Quaker pamphleteering fueled partly by the collapse of Richard Cromwell's Protectorate in April and the restoration of the Rump in May – both a result of revolutionary pressure from the Army.[57] While Fox's text does not refer explicitly to the political events of that year of crisis, it does convey a sense of apocalyptic excitement as it proclaims the warring Lamb's victory over "the false prophets, Beast and Dragon" now that the "Lord Jesus Christ has come to reign."[58] This fiercely anticlerical and millenarian text becomes the occasion for Fox to pour out his sweeping condemnation of church and state authorities in a long series of provocative rhetorical questions rich in apocalyptic references. Asserting his own prophetic agency, Fox assumes a militant posture as the "Officer" of the Lamb entrusted by God to issue forth the "Lambs Message . . . in this his day which is come."[59] An impassioned monologue and a work of sustained apocalypticism, Fox's visionary work achieves its exhortative force, however, through a different kind of repetition than Fox usually employs in his earlier tracts. He punctuates his flood of rhetorical questions and apocalyptic themes in *The Lambs Officer* by his constant refrain of "Guilty, or not guilty?" – a provocative question he poses to priests, magistrates, earthly kings, as well as other Antichristian powers, as he imagines them all being brought not before the courts of the nation but before the "Judgement Bar" of the Lamb itself and compelled to drink "the cup of the indignation of the Almighty" (see Rev. 14:10). Altogether Fox repeats this accusatory question, or a variation upon it, over fifty times throughout this tract of twenty-two pages; and sometimes he repeats the question as many as five times per page. Frequent, too, is Fox's refrain that these worldly powers have all drunk the great Whore's cup – "do you not drink it daily?" he asks[60] – and given themselves up to the power of the Beast and Dragon. Such insistent repetition of accusatory questions creates the emotional concentration of Fox's prophetic tract and heightens its dramatic forcefulness.

After narrating for a page and a half, at the beginning of his text, a history of Antichristian power – an account of the Dragon giving his power to the Beast, the Beast making war with the saints, the earthly kings drinking the great whore's wine, and the whore as the persecuting power then drinking the blood of the prophets, martyrs, and saints – the visionary Fox launches into his lengthy series of thundering rhetorical questions. These denounce the professional, university-trained ministers of his age and link them with the flourishing powers of Antichrist:

> And did not you stand in the day of the Beasts power, when he killed
> the Saints, and made War with them, the true Ministers?. . . . And did

while evoking too the righteous rider of Revelation 19:11–16 – Christ
who descends from heaven to earth mounted on a white horse followed by
his conquering angelic armies mounted in a similar fashion. Indeed, Fox's
passage combines the two apocalyptic horsemen of Revelation 6:2 and
19:11, since the first is armed with a bow (not mentioned by Fox) and the
other with a sword which issues out of his mouth. Fox's vision of the
victorious scene at the end of time evokes not only the messianic wedding
of the Lamb (in Rev. 19:7), symbolic here of the union between the Lamb
and the faithful saints (the godly creation and true church), but also the
militant apocalyptic passage which envisions the warrior Lamb
vanquishing the Beast, the false prophet, the kings of the earth as well as
other forces of Antichrist: 'And the remnant were slain with the sword of
Him that sat upon the horse, which sword proceeded out of his mouth'
(Rev. 19:21). As 'the King of kings, and the Lord of lords' (see Rev.
19:16, cf. 1:5), the conquering Lamb will have sovereignty over all earthly
rulers and powers – 'for now.' Fox announces to them at the end of his
apocalyptic monologue, 'is your time and day of judgment.' Such
eschatological passages of writing by Fox, infused with the rhetoric of the
Lamb. Were inspired by Revelation and reinvigorated by a new spirit of the
Spirit give Fox's revolutionary prose its sense of exhilaration and urgent
expectation.

One could of course highlight numerous ... rich passages of sublime
apocalyptic writing from the revolutionary pamphlets of Fox's
interregnum years. A pressing sense of living 'in the last times,' as he
actively proclaimed that the terrible day of the Lord's wrath was
imminent, clearly stimulated the verbal and rhetorical powers of this
Lamb's prophetic officer. As he poured out his fiery apocalyptic texts
... of these emerging years ('Quaker writing,' Fox managed to revitalize
... of the scriptural language, metaphors ... myths ... that they indeed
... had fresh eschatological meanings and become potent weapons with
which to alarm the nation and warn the trembling Whore of the Lamb.

... apocalyptic ... Frank ... Early Modern ...
... (London: 1658); see Hugh Barbour, The Quakers in Puritan England
... (New Haven: Yale University Press, 1964) 1, 40, who notes the frequency of biblical allusions in
Quaker texts; and Geoffrey F. Nuttall, Christianity and Violence (Wallingford: Pendle Hill Press,
1972) 12–13, 38. References to the Bible are to the King James version.
... The conquering Lamb derives from Revelation, while the Lamb of meekness derives ... from

LIVERPOOL JOHN MOORES UNIVERSITY
LEARNING SERVICES

Morgan ... Rel ... and Feminist Literary History: A "Mother in Israel" Calls to the Jews

JUDITH KEGAN ... MBER

other Old Testament matriarchs, to prophets who warned straying Jewry to return to their covenant, and to apostles and evangelists who preached and wrote letters spreading the word of Christ's mission.

Fell was the first Quaker to address the Jews, an interest she manifested in the 1650s in a period when Cromwell was considering readmitting Jews to England for the first time since they were expelled in the year 1290.[17] Seventeenth-century England saw a brief florescence of "philo-semitism," a confluence of scholarly, religious, and mercantile interests. Some scholars, including the upper-class philosopher Anne Conway, a late-life convert to Quakerism , delved into Jewish mysticism or the occult. Others sought to advance Hebrew scholarship and thought that the original language spoken in Eden was Hebrew. Millenarians believed that the imminent prologue to Christ's second coming would be the conversion of the Jews, which the poet Andrew Marvell so memorably mocked. In addition, English proponents of readmission argued that good economic reasons favored allowing Jewish overseas traders into England. However, as David Katz summarizes, "these English philo-semites wanted Hebrew without tears, philo-semitism without Jews."[18]

Despite the modest changes wrought by philo-semitism in early modern England, popular and learned representations of Jews continued to present them as deceitful, treacherous, dirty, and evil to the point of diabolism.[19] Such negative stereotypes are most familiar to us through plays like Marlowe's *Jew of Malta* and Shakespeare's *Merchant of Venice*. Dympna Callaghan records the racialization of ancient Palestine in Elizabeth Cary's closet drama, *The Tragedy of Mariam: Fair Queen of Jewry*, in which the tragic Hebrew heroine is described as physically pale, white, and beautiful, as well as morally and spiritually superior to the dark and lustful Salome, a comparison through which Mariam's sufferings may recall Christ's, while Salome's murderous duplicity recalls that of Christ-killing Jews.[20] Late twentieth-century feminist scholarship is particularly interested in such intersections of gender with other hierarchical social categories, whereas earlier feminist critics focused more simply on Fell as a champion of women's rights. When Fell wrote, English imperialism and the slave trade were becoming consolidated, and racialization, class division, and gender roles were becoming more polarized without having yet attained their modern forms. In this atmosphere, Quakers like Fell stand out as early abolitionists and defenders of women's rights. "God is no respecter of persons," Fell stressed (232).[21] In *The Call of the Seed of Israel* directed to contemporary Jews, she writes, "the same Lord brings from Egypt, and out of the house of bondage still. Therefore all people, high and low, rich and poor, Jews and gentiles, Barbarian, Scythian, mind the light" (470–71).

Quite soon after her own conversion, Fell apparently felt called to participate in the course of Christian history moving toward Christ's second coming, a story in which the conversion of the Jews formed a crucial and penultimate chapter. The first preachings by Fox that Fell heard, which so impressed her, depended on the distinction between the "Jew outward" and the "Jew inward" as images of perfunctory and genuine faith.[22] This imagery permeates Fell's addresses to Jews and seems to operate for her both as a set of universal analogies and, like the Bible, as literally applicable description: "Yea all the prophets from Samuel . . . have likewise foretold of these days," she wrote to the Jews; "ye are the children of the prophets, and of the covenant" (477). Fell proselytized the Jews with a sense of urgency, rushing to publish in order to circumvent Judge Fell's disapproval of his wife's appearance in print and seeking to have her work translated into Latin, Hebrew, and Dutch for distribution among continental Jewry.[23]

Although she was a dualist who divided the world into two contrasted groups, Friends with the inner light and all others, Fell was not sexist or racist in the modern sense of these terms; rather, she believed that people from all social categories were capable of salvation. In short, vigorous phrases, she urged the Jews:

> So turn to the light, believe in the light, and wait in the light, to receive the promise; for there is neither Jew nor Greek, there is neither bond nor free, there is neither male nor female, that doth believe in the light. . . but they are all one in Christ Jesus. . . .then are they Abraham's seed, and heirs . . . (487–8).

This apparent egalitarianism uses metaphors that assimilate contemporary Christians to historical Jews, "Abraham's seed, and heirs." Though this discourse is not racist, it is unquestioningly ethnocentric in assuming the truth and superiority of the Friends' English version of Christianity. She views her own interpretations of scripture and history as complete, correct, self-evident, and sufficient as a source of spiritual authority; for instance, she says, "I am clearly convinced, and am assured" by the voice of God she hears within herself that bishops are not according to God's laws (359).[24] She addresses *Certain Queries to the Teachers and Rabbis among the Jews*: "What the way of holiness is, and where it is, where the unclean cannot pass?" she asks them, and "Whose kingdom is an everlasting kingdom?" She cites the Old Testament to them and then demands, "answer these queries, according to the law and prophets" (190–91), as though her Christian answers to these questions must be obvious.[25] She evidences no knowledge that traditional Jewish exegesis provided alternative answers to such queries that an effective polemicist should acknowledge and refute.

Fell can be caustic, especially to those in positions of authority like the bishops and judges who persecuted Quakers. However, her tone toward contemporary Jews was unusually conciliatory. She was unlikely ever to have seen a living Jew when she began her polemics; the small crypto-Jewish presence in England was concentrated in London. Instead, she seems to have been influenced by a reading of the Bible that saw past types being fulfilled in the present so that Quakers often stood in the place of Old Testament Jews, especially the prophets. Along with virtually all other Christians in her age, Fell considered post-Biblical Jews unusually obtuse, "faithless and unbelieving still going on in hardness of heart" not to have realized that Jesus was their messiah (173). However, she does not see them as inherently prone to evil or diabolic, nor does she blame them for killing Christ as Fox did.[26] Other Quakers, including her former servant William Caton, wrote of the Jews as religiously benighted and as unscrupulous in business dealings with Christians.[27] Fell portrays Jews less as depraved adults than as disobedient children, "stiff-necked and uncircumcized in hearts and ears, who are disobedient to their measures of grace" and "rebellious and stubborn, children of Ephraim" who "refused to walk" in God's laws (470, 471). Because of the Jews' "provocations, who always rebelled against Him," God turned to the gentiles, she explains, and gentile salvation, through a kind of sibling rivalry between Christians and Jews, should now provoke the Jews to return to God's favor. Like prodigal children, "now, that your stumbling hath been the riches of the . . . gentiles, how much more will your gathering be joy" (188). For Fell, the Jews' special role in redemption continues into the English present: "now let all people try and search, whether all the priests and teachers" of England have not forgotten "the righteous law of God, which endures for ever . . .this they call a covenant of works, and say, Christ hath abolished it, which is contrary to Christ's own words" for Christ was sent "not to destroy, but to fulfill this law" (472).

Fell read contemporary English life in terms of Biblical narrative, understanding her present world as the literal enactment of figures from the Biblical past: the creation of man and woman in God's image, Abraham's faith and God's promise to his "seed," the prophets' denunciation of their people's wickedness, and the Psalmist's laments over the captivity of Zion in the Old Testament and Jesus' parables in the New Testament. She saw the Quakers as latter-day Biblical Hebrews, a righteous minority in captivity to a worldly majority. When she wrote *The Call to the Seed of Israel* in Lancaster jail, she was a literal captive for her controversial religious beliefs. She spoke of herself and other Friends as included among the "seed of Abraham" to whom God's promises had been made, and in her writings she spoke as a prophet to her wicked and unbelieving land, as an apostle to those superficial Christians who behaved like Biblical Pharisees, and as an evangelist to the ignorant and unbelieving.

Fell's appellation by other Quakers as a "mother in Israel" assimilated her to the prophet Deborah, to the virtuous woman of Proverbs, and to the Old Testament matriarchs. Fell repeatedly cited Old Testament women like Deborah and Miriam as exemplary for Friends. Two of her daughters were named for Old Testament matriarchs – Sarah, who ran the household at Swarthmoor Hall for many years, and Rachel, born and named after her mother's conversion. Thus Fell and other Quakers often represented themselves as good Jews among backsliders and unbelievers and as "the people of God, (who by the world are called Quakers)," a divinely chosen minority with a mission of cosmic significance.[28] This historical view thus superimposed Pentateuch, prophetic, and New Testament time onto the English seventeenth century in one master narrative through which the Quakers remained God's people while occupying the roles of Old Testament Jews, New Testament Jewish Christians, and modern gentiles reprimanding contemporary Jewish backwardness. Because Fell believed that the Jews would convert to Christianity, they were still part of God's saving plan for humanity and therefore ultimately in alliance with the Quakers, who were "the people of God" in the present age. This quality of Quaker thought has been called "logically static," leading to a sense of "timelessness," and manifesting itself in alogical, "incantatory" prose.[29] Yet Fell's discourses depend not on timelessness but on the belief that a specific, divinely adumbrated future time is visible in the present. Therefore, the Jews' coming conversion and salvation, foretold in the Bible, encourages Christians now to treat them in terms of their future, more satisfactory role among the saved. Through such beliefs Fell attains a millenarian and utopian kind of egalitarianism that cuts across and so calls into question our racial as well as class and gender categories. She addresses people who are divided socially in the present in terms of the one Biblical history they have already shared and of the equality before Christ they will eventually share. Her own "voice," then, comes to be heard in her appropriation and refiguration of the Biblical imagery and rhetoric she assumes to be universally applicable to all people and situations. Her prose superimposes several historical periods and their divine purposes upon one another and weaves Biblical quotations seamlessly into her own, using Biblical genres like prophecy and epistle, Biblical imagery, and Biblical modes of address, including the promising and admonitory second person and the authoritative first person of the Lord's speaking through His prophets. Fell saw Biblical imagery becoming literal truth before her eyes: "the figures, and the types, and the shadows are ceased," she tells the Jews (124). Previously, their Mosaic law, circumcision, Sabbath, and other distinctive observances "were outward, and the Temple . . . was outward; these were figures, types, and shadows of him, who was to come," the Christ who has now arrived (480). Thus the figurative is also outside of and prior to a truth that is now present and inward in her and other Quakers, and from which her voice authoritatively speaks.

Repeatedly Fell contrasts a unified center of divine spirit in the believer's heart with an alienation from God figured in Biblical history as the scattering or dispersal of peoples: Christ the gatherer was dividing his followers from the unbelievers, and God was now sending "to bring his seed out of bondage, and out of the house of darkness, from under Pharoah" (70). Fell claims that Christ "is now come, and coming to redeem Israel, and to divide the Red Sea, and to overturn Pharoah and his host" (71).[30] Ultimately, Christ will gather and reunite all his people: "for Jews and Gentiles, barbarians, Scythians, bond and free," Christ "hath taken down the partition-wall betwixt us, and hath made of twain, one new man" (478).

Fell often figured the state of alienation from God as a prison, or "house of darkness," or decrepit house. She reports that one night she "lay upon my bed and saw a vision of the professions of the world . . . as a long, torn, rotten house, so shatter'd, and so like to fall" that it roused her to pity (90).[31] Such imagery resonates with Fell's status as a wealthy head of household. Although her explicit ideology appears to be socially egalitarian, we can also see the ways that her status in society encouraged her self-assurance, just as her religious imagery echoed her pride in her position as an independent homeowner, as when she demanded of a persecuting judge, "What law have I broken by worshipping God in my own house?"[32] The same sense of ownership was manifested in her statement to the magistrates who had imprisoned George Fox in 1660, "I am concerned in the thing, inasmuch as he was apprehended in my house."[33]

Protestations of equality made by those who enjoy the advantages of race and class privilege also characterize twentieth-century middle-class white feminists, according to their critics. These critics also charge that the interdependent "voices" and maternal empathy championed by mainstream modern feminists can be similarly imperialistic in assuming that they understand all women's best interests and that all other women will achieve unity around these feminists' goals rather than their own.[34]

Fell seems liable to a similar charge when she writes, with perfect confidence, that she is a reliable measure for others and that unity with them will be achieved on her terms: "this I was moved of the Lord to write to you, in love and tenderness to the measure of God in you, with which I have unity" (73).[35] Fell's social egalitarianism, her empathy, and her self assurance can be analyzed in terms of these modern feminist debates. At the same time, historicizing the terms of such debates illuminates Fell's significant accomplishments within the Society of Friends and early modern England.

Fell's empathy was particularly unusual with regard to the Jews. The opening lines of her tracts to the Jews reverberate with imagery of her and God's "call" to them and with imagery of union and gathering. The earliest of these tracts begins: "for Manesseth-ben-Israel: the call of the Jews out of Babylon, which is good tidings to the meek, liberty to the captives, and of opening of prison doors. To the Jewish and Hebrew nation, who are scattered up and down the face of the earth" (101). Next is "A Loving Salutation to the Seed of Abraham among the Jews, wherever they are scattered up and down upon the face of the earth. . . . that ye may . . . be brought to the fold where there is one shepherd, and one sheepfold" (152–3) and where God "will return and gather thee from all nations" into England, "the good land, where there is one heart, and one spirit, where the Lord is one, and his name one, and this is the land of promise, and the covenant of God unto you, and all nations" (182). In 1668 Fell figures contemporary Jewry as the sorrowing woman of the Psalms, a fallen "daughter of Sion," when she writes "A Call unto the Seed of Israel, that they may come out of Egypt's darkness, and house of bondage, unto the land of rest. . . . Awake, awake, put on thy strength O Zion, put on thy beautiful garments O Jerusalem. . . ," a usage that permits Fell to address unknown Jews as though she is a woman speaking compassionately to another woman who is in trouble (467–8).[36]

Fell is remarkable in these tracts not only for the relative sympathy with which she addresses the Jews but also for her rhetorical voice – intimate, persuasive, cajoling even in reprimand, as when she chides, "do not always hate to be reformed" (186). She is also capable of combining intimacy with authority: "I charge thee Manesseh ben Israel, as thou wilt answer it before the living God, that thou let this be read and published among thy brethren" (123). This voice achieves intimacy as well as Biblical resonance from its use of apostrophe and other forms of second person direct address, modulating from the imperative just cited to the repeated language of salutation and "call," with its resonance of divine mission, authority, and vocation. Since the voice of God within assures Quaker faith, this figure of speech is spiritually self-authorizing. For

example, Fell introduces her "Epistles" saying, "Friendly reader, the
following epistles were written at the first appearance of truth among us.
. . . And we were moved of the Lord to write often to Friends. . . ."; she
urges the reader to "cleave to the blessed light" of God's truth, "and it will
lead thee in the path that we have gone, and then thou wilt see, and feel,
and understand what we have gone through; and thou wilt come to be a
witness of the living God. . . ." [37] Thus Fell authorizes her voice and
writings as parallel with those of the evangelists and apostles among
whom Christian truth first appeared centuries earlier, and she implies that
she is equally obligated with these canonical predecessors to call others to
the truth.

"Voice" is a contested issue in feminist literary history. Some use the
term as correlative with women's autonomy, so that women "coming to
voice" make women's history progress, and many scholars discuss early
modern women's strategies for speech in a culture that told them to be
"chaste, silent, and obedient." [38] Several recent books on seventeenth-
century women writers highlight the concept of "voice." For example,
Marilyn Williamson looks for "a definite female voice in women's
poetry" in her study entitled *Raising Their Voices*, and Tina Krontiris'
Oppositional Voices celebrates women's writing as a "study of female
assertiveness" against a dominant ideology that gave women "no legal
rights, no public voice, and certainly no literary voice" outside of religion
and domesticity. [39] Similarly, Charlotte Otten aims to uncover "the lives of
women whose voices were buried," including Fell, in her *English
Women's Voices*. [40] One strategy that many early modern women used to
participate in literature and public culture was emphasizing their own
selflessness and passivity before the will of God that spoke through them.
Conversely, the female prophet might be condemned for self-will,
misguided enthusiasm, or a genuine but passing inspiration that gave
women no lasting credibility. [41] Fell's strategy is somewhat different: by
adopting as her own the voice of a Biblical prophet or "mother in Israel,"
she anchors her writings not in passing inspiration but in the permanent
texts of accepted Christian faith.

Fell's *Loving Salutation* illustrates the way that she creates and
authorizes her own "voice" as she hails or calls the Jews, her addresses to
them reciprocating her own calling within her community as a "mother in
Israel." Fell addresses the Jews saying: "David saith, the fool said in his
heart, there is no God; they are corrupt (Psalms 14, 53). Here you may
see and read your selves where you are, who are out of the way of peace,
and the way of truth, and the life" (152). Thus Fell says that King David
says that the fool says that there is no God, and she directs the Jews to
"read" themselves in the fool's heart, in which God is not, and then to

recoil from this mirror of disbelief in order to "read" their true selves in God's, David's, and her text, which should reverberate in their hearts. Fell chides the Jews to believe her Christian message as they would believe their own Old Testament. Repeatedly, she insists that doubting her words means rejecting their own traditions: "see now whether ye will believe Moses, and whether ye will be obedient to the prophet, that the Lord is raising, like unto Moses, (which is Light) to which, if ye will be obedient, it will gather you from all nations whither you are scattered" (181–2).

To persuade the Jews of their potentially happy role in this grand scenario, Fell shifts from the voice of a Biblical prophet to the voice of immediate divine presence: "here is the large infinite love of God manifested; who saith . . . I will also give thee for a light to the gentiles . . . so think it not strange, to receive this testimony from the gentiles, who have obtained mercy, and received the promise of the Lord, according to Isaiah's prophecy" (187, Isaiah 65). As a gentile giving testimony, Fell aligns herself and so authorizes her text with Old Testament prophecy and with the empathic presumption that she voices not her own will but their benefit through God's "large infinite love." Triumphantly Fell tells the prodigal Jews that if they return to the fold, "kings shall be thy nursing fathers, and their queens thy nursing mothers, they shall bow down to thee with their faces towards the earth, and lick up the dust of thy feet. See here now if this be not fulfilled: is there not even a bowing down unto thee in this loving invitation. . . ." (189). Strikingly, Fell's tract itself fulfills Biblical prophecy, the "bowing down" to the Jews promised in her "loving invitation," her very tone of humility and empathy with the Jews' dispersal a proof of the prophetic inevitability of her message. Having established this identity between her voice and the voice of Biblical truth, Fell then expands her solicitation from first person singular to plural to represent the community of believers that awaits the Jewish converts: "our souls' desire is that you might all be gathered, and come into the covenant of light, and love, and partake with us of the everlasting riches and inheritance that never fades away" (189).

Having attempted throughout her text to call the Jews of contemporary Europe into the inner circle of Christian light, Fell ends by moving away from empathic identification with them in order to position herself as already more truly an inhabitant of the spiritual Israel than are the Jews, its literal descendents, and also as one of its prophets. "[T]he redeemer is coming to Zion," she tells the Jews, "and unto them that turn from transgression in Jacob. So as you turn from your transgression this ye will see, and witness. And so whether you hear or forbear, this shall be an eternal testimony for the Lord, forever. M.F." (189). The secular Renaissance male writer can boast of an eternal and immortalizing art: "so long lives this, and this gives life to thee."[42] Fell, instead, grounds her claims to artistic eternity on the coincidence among the divine word, her religious experience, her own polemical prose, and the historical and transhistorical events of the redemption. All "this ye will see," she claims, and "this" that they will see and may hear then becomes her own "eternal testimony," the tract as they read it. Fell is called to call others through incorporating and personifying the call of God to a people, a calling through which she places herself and her signature for eternity: "This shall be an eternal testimony for the Lord forever. M.F."

Feminist theorist and literary historian Catherine Belsey cites Fell's *Women's Speaking Justified* as evidence that "women had found a voice" in seventeenth-century England, and she connects this voice with the creation of bourgeois subjectivity: "loving partners, specialists in domesticity, nurturing, caring mothers, [women] progressively became autonomous, unified, knowing authors of their own choices" and so came to be liberal subjects who "find a place – in the home, in the bosom of the family" at the "price" of "exclusion from the political."[43] In another work, Belsey explains the idea propounded by Louis Althusser that "people 'recognize' (misrecognize) themselves in the ways in which ideology 'interpellates' them, or in other words, addresses them as subjects, calls them by their names and in turn 'recognizes' their autonomy"; "ideology interpellates concrete individuals as subjects" so that they become the "subjects who work by themselves" necessary to the functioning of a capitalist society.[44] However, I have been arguing that seventeenth-century Quaker discourses provided alternative ways of calling or "interpellating" people. Although early Friends, including Fell, did adopt some apparently capitalist business practices, the concepts of the rise of capitalism and bourgeois liberalism do not adequately account for Quaker radical inwardness and discourse in the mid-seventeenth century. Neither can such discourse be simply assimilated to the model of feminist progress that looks only to more women finding more public and louder "voices" on behalf of women.

Margaret Fell's authorial voice is created by her calling and by what and whom she calls. The ineffable experiences of being divinely called, the workings of the spirit within the believer, were translated by early Friends in accordance with discourses and practices that made such experience intelligible. For Fell, being called a "mother in Israel" was part of a discursive context through which she shaped and understood her experience and her evangelical impulses. The theory of interpellation says that we are what we are called, hailed into place by the discourses that name us, "subjected" beings who submit to authority.[45] Cultural feminism says that we are what we call or hail others, that women gain subjectivity through voice, through women speaking to one another and through criticizing their male-dominated societies. I have suggested here that Margaret Fell creates a voice for herself as she calls others and as she is called by others, especially as a "mother in Israel." This title condenses many of the possibilities for identification within early Quaker discourses; it allowed Fell to place herself as an authoritative figure speaking in print about public national and international political and religious issues like the readmission of the Jews to England and the second coming of Christ. Although Fell was undoubtedly bolstered in confidence by her unusual position as a wealthy Northern landowner, the rhetorical position she assumes is not simply that of a capitalist individual or a bourgeois feminist. Rather, one of the historical possibilities opened to her in the English mid-seventeenth century is that of assuming an apparently transhistorical position through the belief that the events of Old Testament Israel were paralleled and fulfilled in contemporary England. Strikingly, Fell early and repeatedly addressed extensive theological and polemical works to the Jews of contemporary Europe, adopting toward them an empathic, maternal, and prophetic rhetoric. These works, then, served not only Fell's explicit millenarian ideology about the Jews' role in advancing Christ's second coming, but they also functioned to expand the possibilities latent in Quaker Biblical usage and discourses so that Fell could create for herself an authorial position corresponding to her prophetic, authoritative, and female-gendered "calling" as a "mother in Israel."

NOTES

1. Hugh Barbour and Arthur O. Roberts, eds., *Early Quaker Writings 1650–1700* (Grand Rapids: William B. Eerdmans, 1973), 477. I have modernized spelling and capitalization in all quotations. Throughout this essay I call its subject Margaret Fell.
2. Rachel Fell quoted by Bonnelyn Young Kunze, *Margaret Fell and the Rise of Quakerism* (Stanford: Stanford University Press, 1994), 233–4; "A Testimony from Margaret Fell's Children" in Margaret Fell, *A Brief Collection of Remarkable Passages and Occurrences Relating to the Birth, Education, Life, Conversion, Travels, Services, and Deep Sufferings of that Ancient, Eminent, and Faithful Servant of the Lord Margaret Fell . . .* (London: J. Sowle, 1710), A1. Quotations from Fell's work will be cited from this volume parenthetically in the text hereafter, with spelling and capitalization modernized. Fell's manuscripts I have seen are more lightly punctuated and capitalized than this edition. I thank the Friends House Library, London, for access to these manuscripts. Other early Quaker women were also called "mothers in Israel." For example, Theophila Townsend so refers to Jane Whitehead in *A Testimony Concerning the life and Death of Jane Whitehead, Concerning her Sufferings*, by T.T. (1676), Friends Library Quaker Tracts, vol.51, no.25.
3. *For Manasseth*, 101–24; *Loving Salutation*, 152–89; *Call Seed*, 467–92, *Brief Collection*. Kunze dates *The Loving Salutation* 1656 or 1657, 211–12. I do not discuss here the possible differences in Fell's attitudes to the date of the Second Coming among these tracts.
4. I allude here to the concept of "interpellation," a calling or hailing that is said to fix an individual's subjectivity within the social contexts of a given historical culture; see Louis Althusser, *Lenin and Philosophy and Other Essays*, trans. Ben Brewster (London: New Left Books, 1971), 169–83.

5. Margaret George, *Women in the First Capitalist Society: Experiences in Seventeenth-Century England* (Urbana and Chicago: University of Illinois Press, 1988), 93. For Fell's biography, see Kunze; also Isabell Ross, *Margaret Fell: Mother of Quakerism* (London and New York: Longman, Green, 1949).

6. See my earlier discussion of Fell's writings, "Re-Gendering Individualism: Margaret Fell Fox and Quaker Rhetoric," in *Privileging Gender in Early Modern England*, ed. Jean R. Brink (Kirksville, Mo: Sixteenth Century Journal Publishers, 1993), 205–24. Feminist literary historians have been most concerned with Fell's *Women's Speaking Justified*, reprinted in Publication #194 (UCLA: William Andrews Clark Memorial Library, 1979); Moira Ferguson, ed., *First Feminists: British Women Writers 1578-1799* (Bloomington: Indiana University Press; Old Westbury: Feminist Press, 1985), 114–27; and Charlotte F. Otten, ed., *English Women's Voices, 1540-1700* (Miami: Florida International University Press, 1992), 363–78.

7. Many of these epistles are published in the *Brief Collection*. For the importance of women's manuscript writings generally, and Fell's epistles particularly, see Margaret J.M. Ezell, *Writing Women's Literary History* (Baltimore and London: Johns Hopkins University Press, 1993), esp. 144–5.

8. Ross; Kunze, esp. 8, 229.

9. For example, Mary Howgill wrote her, "Dear Mother in the everlasting fountain of life. . ," Friends' Library Swarthmore Manuscripts vol.2, no.493. Rachel Abraham replied to Fell's "kind motherly advice about suckling my children" in 1684, Friends House Library, Spence manuscript vol.3, no.188.

10. *The Examination and Tryall of Margaret Fell and George Fox . . . at Lancaster*, 1664.

11. James Nayler letter, Friends House Library, Swarthmore ms, vol.2, no.895,.

12. See Ross; also Margaret Hope Bacon, *Mothers of Feminism: The Story of Quaker Women in America* (San Francisco: Harper and Row, 1986).

13. Lerner, *The Creation of Feminist Consciousness from the Middle-Ages to Eighteen-seventy* (New York and Oxford: Oxford University Press, 1993), 101. Margaret Olofson Thickstun cites Fell to show that "the literary presentation of women in English narratives changed dramatically during the seventeenth century," *Fictions of the Feminine: Puritan Doctrine and the Representation of Women* (Ithaca and London: Cornell University Press, 1988), 1.

14. For example, Fell addressed Fox as "our dear nursing father," Ross 36–7. For medieval women's religious imagery, see Caroline Walker Bynum, "'. . . And Woman His Humanity': Female Imagery in the Religious Writing of the Later Middle Ages," *Gender and Religion: On the Complexity of Symbols*, ed. by Caroline Walker Bynum, Steven Harrell, and Paula Richman (Boston: Beacon Press, 1986), 257–88.

15. Kunze, 224.

16. See Sara Ruddick, *Maternal Thinking: Toward a Politics of Peace* (Beacon Press: Boston, 1989); and Gardiner, "Re-Gendering Individualism."

17. Kunze, 5; Ross, 5.

18. Anne Conway, letters to Henry More 29 Nov. 1675 and 4 Feb. 1675/76 discuss her conversion, *The Conway Letters: The Correspondence of Anne, Viscountess Conway, Henry More, and Their Friends 1642-1684*, rev. ed. by Marjorie Hope Nicolson and Sarah Hutton (Oxford: Clarendon Press, 1992), 407–9, 420–23. Fell writes of Conway's conversion in 1678, in a letter to Katherine Evans, Friends Library, Spence mss., vol.378, no.12. For Conway's philosophy, see Anne Conway, *The Principles of the Most Ancient and Modern Philosophy*, intro. Peter Loptson (The Hague, Boston, London: Martinus Nijhoff, 1982); David S. Katz, *Philo-Semitism and the Readmission of the Jews to England 1603-1655* (Oxford: Clarendon Press, 1982), 244. Katz quotes Thomas Carlyle calling the philo-semite Thomas Tany "seemingly a kind of Quaker," 117.

19. See John Edwards, *The Jews in Christian Europe 1400–1700* (London and New York: Routledge, 1988); Jonathan I. Israel, *European Jewry in the Age of Mercantilism 1550–1750*, 2nd ed. (Oxford: Clarendon Press, 1989).

20. Dympna Callaghan, "Re-Reading Elizabeth Cary's *The Tragedie of Mariam, Faire Queene of Jewry*," in *Women, "Race," and Writing in the Early Modern Period*, ed. Margo Hendricks and Patricia Parker (London and New York: Routledge, 1994), 163–77. I extend Callaghan's comparison.

21. *An Evident Demonstration to God's Elect. . ., 1660, Brief Collection*, 220–32. The doctrine of spiritual equality is often asserted by other early Quakers as well.
22. Kunze, 218.
23. Margaret Fell letter, 1657, Friends' Library, Spence mss, vol.378, no.49. Kunze discusses the printing and distribution of the tracts and a possible connection with Spinoza, 212–15.
24. *A Touchstone: or a Trial by the Scriptures. . ., 1666, Brief Collection*, 357–457.
25. *Certain Queries to the Teachers and Rabbis among the Jews, 1657, Brief Collection*, 190–92.
26. Kunze, 223–4.
27. Kunze, 215–16.
28. *Evident Demonstration*, 237.
29. Jackson I. Cope, "Seventeenth-Century Quaker Style," *PMLA* 71 (1956): 725–54, pp.734, 744; also see Richard Bauman, *Let Your Words Be Few: Symbolism of Speaking and Silence among Seventeenth-Century Quakers* (Cambridge: Cambridge University Press, 1983).
30. "A General Epistle, of Margaret Fell, to Friends," 1655, *Brief Collection*, 70–73.
31. "To All the Professors of the World," 1656, *Brief Collection*, 73–91.
32. *Examination and Tryall.*
33. Quoted in *The Journal of George Fox*, rev. ed. by John L. Nickalls (Cambridge: Cambridge University Press, 1952), 383. The issue is somewhat parallel to Fell's failure to wear plain clothing; she kept to the belief that "outward things" did not matter while continuing to wear the clothing of her class that might impress others.
34. Many cultural feminist critics base their view of women's empathy and voice on Carol Gilligan, *In a Different Voice: Psychological Theory and Women's Development* (Cambridge: Harvard University Press, 1982). For a general critique of cultural feminist literary critics, see Chela Sandoval, "U.S. Third World Feminism: The Theory and Method of Oppositional Consciousness in the Postmodern World," *Genders*, 10, (1991): 1–24; for a critique specifically of mainstream feminist scholarship on women writers of early modern England, see Margaret W. Ferguson, "Moderation and its Discontents: Recent Work on Renaissance Women," *Feminist Studies* 20.2 (Summer 1994): 349–66.
35. "A General Epistle. . . ."
36. Fell repeats the figure in her tract *The Daughter of Sion Awakened . . ., 1677, Brief Collection*, 509–30.
37. *Brief Collection*, 45–7.
38. Suzanne Hull, *Chaste, Silent and Obedient: English Books for Women 1475–1640* (San Marino: Huntington Library, 1982).
39. Marilyn Williamson, *Raising Their Voices: British Women Writers, 1650–1750* (Detroit: Wayne State University Press, 1990), 18; Tina Krontiris, *Oppositional Voices: Women as Writers and Translators of Literature in the English Renaissance* (London and New York: Routledge, 1992), 8, 141.
40. Otten, xv.
41. This 17th-century condemnation is documented by Phyllis Mack, "Women as Prophets during the English Civil War," *Feminist Studies* 8.1 (Spring 1982): 19–46, 38. Mack gives a more comprehensive discussion of Quaker women's roles in *Visionary Women: Ecstatic Prophecy in Seventeenth-Century England* (Berkeley: University of California Press, 1992). Christine Trevett notes that Fell "did not follow the model of the prophetess, whose temporary state of inspiration alone validated her public activity," *Women and Quakerism in the Seventeenth Century* (York: Ebor Press, 1991), 55. Elaine Hobby differentiates Fell's "judicious, rational presentation" and "tone of clear authority" from the "fervour" of other Quaker visionaries, *Virtue of Necessity: English Women's Writing 1649–88* (Ann Arbor: University of Michigan Press, 1988).
42. Shakespeare, sonnet 18.
43. Catherine Belsey, *The Subject of Tragedy: Identity and Difference in Renaissance Drama* (London and New York: Methuen, 1985), 219, 192–3.
44. Belsey, *Critical Practice* (London and New York: Methuen, 1980), 61, 64, 67.
45. Belsey, *Critical Practice*, 62.

Hidden Things Brought to Light:
Enthusiasm and Quaker Discourse

NIGEL SMITH

The prose pamphlets of the radicals during the English Civil War and Interregnum have recently been admired for their verve, their unusual means of challenging authority and their sheer novelty.[1] What, then, does radical prose in the English Revolution do? The pamphlets that we most readily think of (those, for instance, of the Levellers and the Diggers) were developments of established traditions in petitioning, controversy and popular satire. To this extent, it may be argued that they offered little new in their forms, despite the novelty of the political and religious ideas voiced in them. Yet more than this, the prose of the radicals also came to reorganize categories of divinity, self or subjectivity and cosmos. Radicals rewrote notions of selfhood, society and divinity in a number of striking, sometimes bizarre ways, in which their modes of expression were intrinsic to their ideas. To this extent, the prose styles of the radicals were truly revolutionary, and represent a practical literary response that we should situate between conservative assertions of natural and divinely sanctioned hierarchies, and the never-never-land of the utopian tradition, which itself is often (quite wrongly) connected to the radical texts.[2]

How does Quaker writing fit into this spectrum? When Jacques Derrida wrote that a (literary) genre is in some sense a part of its author, he spoke with particular relevance to the radicals.[3] For radical prose, Quaker writing and all, functions as a kind of mirror in which the possibilities of praxis or action are elaborated. Or, as we shall see, for the Quakers, discourse not only showed the workings of the inner light but also embodied them. In the general case of radical religion, prophecy stands most centrally as the literary feature linking the world of the text and the world of events and bodies.[4] Since so much early Quaker protest depended upon bodily as well as verbal gesture, body and language were inextricably linked as the sites in which the workings of the inner light were known. And yet Quaker pamphlets and letters, for all their power, stand as the "writing degree zero" on the radical spectrum, for they display none of the extravagant traits of prophetic personality that we see in Ranter pamphlets, and those of associated prophets, or the schemes for reorganizing the world that we see in Digger writing. But it was in this apparently "flat style" that the most astonishing revelations of Quaker identity and vision in this period were embedded.

None of these innovations by Quakers had anything in common with the innovations in public discourse that emerged during the course of the 1640s and 1650s.[5] To some extent other radicals exploited these forms, as was the case with the Levellers. But however often we find Quaker pamphlets in Thomason's bindings, so also Fox and the other early Friends display a consistent hostility to newsbooks. The Quakers were highly sensitive to their misrepresentation in newsbooks (especially those operating under Protectorate sponsorship), and voiced a great sense of victory when newsbook-writing ministers, like Henry Walker, were, in their eyes, confounded. The more extreme Quakers, such as John Penneyman, publicly burned sackfuls of newsbooks well into the Restoration. In this way, Quaker discourse wanted absolutely no part of the "revolution in the public sphere." And yet the Friends were brilliant publicists, and were clearly using subsidized publication, in order to proselytize, from a very early stage.[6]

Some years ago I published a short essay on the early Quaker enthusiast John Perrot, whose work alarmed the Quaker leadership and who was eventually excluded from the movement. In particular I connected his personal behaviour (especially during his imprisonment and torture in Rome between 1658 and 1661) with the extravagant nature of his writings (notably his long poem *A Sea of the Seed's Sufferings*).[7] I received some criticism in reviews for maintaining that Perrot was typical of a "transformation of subjectivity" – the result of the radical religious *diaspora* of the mid-seventeenth-century.[8] I want in this essay to defend that view, and to develop the theme with reference to a number of issues pertaining to the early Quakers and their use of words. The Quaker enthusiasts certainly had a great deal in common with the less enthusiastic Friends, and their split is instructive in illuminating the paradoxes outlined above with regard to the Quaker use of language, and its relationship with other religious radical discourse.

Perrot, James Nayler, and all the other Quaker enthusiasts who fell under Fox's censure had a friend in Robert Rich. Rich's behavior during the punishment of his friend Nayler is an example of the mingling of strange words with strange behavior, and a further example of the extreme Quaker enthusiasm witnessed in Perrot's actions and writings:

> (the next day) there came unto him one *Robert Rich* (so called) who when he was approaching neer him sang, but what it was, I know not: but when he saw *James Nayler*, he saluted him, by bowing to him: and having asked whether he had prayed for him; *James* answered, Yea, he had. Whereupon, this *Rich* took him round the

middle, stroaked his face, and kissed him. And having took his leave of *James Nayler,* he descended the stairs, saying, *Oh ye hard hearted people, and unbelieving Generation, will ye not believe, although ye see such wonders, signs and miracles wrought before ye.*[9]

Robert Rich accompanied him, with confortable words, kisses, and stroakings on his face, until the remainder of Justice was executed; *Nayler* having stood in the pillory till two of the clock . . . *Robert Rich,* through his ardent affection, licked the wound on his forehead. The superscription over his head was, *For HORRID BLASPHEMY, GRAND IMPOSTURE, and SEDUCING OF THE PEOPLE:* which inscription *Robert Rich* endeavoured to smother, by clapping another over it, which was, *THIS IS THE KING OF THE JEWS.*[10]

Rich's actions, like those of Nayler's other followers, bear out an extravagant re-enacting of events surrounding the crucifixion of Christ as described in the New Testament.

Rich, known by the prophetic name of Mordecai, was well born, and lived as a wealthy merchant in London before becoming a convert to Quakerism in 1654. His persecution along with other prominent Quakers at Banbury in the following year does not mark him out as a particularly extreme Friend. Indeed his own contribution to the tract that recounted this episode is remarkably Foxean in its nature, although there was often little between most Quakers and their attitudes at this early stage. But during the Nayler episode in 1656–57, Rich's loyalty to Nayler earned him the "hatred" of the Quakers. While Nayler, his health ruined, and with not long to live, was eventually reconciled to Fox, Rich took another path. As we now know from the scholarship of G.F. Nuttall, Rich eventually withdrew to Barbados, but not before establishing an association of ex-Naylerites and fellow-traveling enthusiasts.[11] He retained correspondence between Nayler, Perrot and Fox, and published it in the later 1670s after he had retreated to Barbados (as Perrot had gone to Jamaica). Like Perrot, Rich combined an extravagant appearance and manners (or so it seemed to other Quakers) with a deep learning. He maintained a close relationship, even across the Atlantic, with the "Church of the First Born," and in particular its prominent figure Robert Bacon, a long-standing religious radical, and guardian of a textual tradition of enthusiasm and "rising above ordinances."[12] Rich himself resolved to adopt no particular *form* of religion, but:

attaining a more universal Spirit, *he found* freedom *in his mind to dive into the several Forms of* Professors *now appearing in this, or* other Lands, *with a design to* cull out *the Gold, (i.e.) that which was good in all, and to reject the Dross.*[13]

Rich himself saw this as a casting away of human inventions like the concept of the Trinity:

> your elaborate distinctions of the three persons in the trinity, at last reduce us but to this verity, which the systems of your several Creeds confirm, *viz.* that these three are one Immortal, Invisible and onely Wise God, and this eternal unity as he multiplies or discovers himself in his several operations, so that he owns himself under various Names, as Father, Son, Spirit, with many other significant appellations, as the Love, the Light, the way, . . . and yet all these intend but one simple undivided and eternal spirit of truth, whereby we are begotten into the life of God, the Image of God, that makes us partakers of the Divine Nature.[14]

Even the Quakers, Rich eventually came to see, along with the other early Quaker schismatics, were guilty of "outward," "formal" religion, although he again expressed this in a language characteristic of early Quakerism:

> Therefore is he now arising to dash the potsherds of the earth one against another, brother against brother, one against two, and two against three, till the earth have disclosed the bloud she hath drunk, and the seed of God be recovered, . . . For this I know and do declare, that my God will not leave overturning, overturning, overturning, till he comes who brings along with him truth and love to iniquity and righteousness, whose right it is to rule and reign in the hearts and consciences of his people.[15]

To this extent, the outward testimonies preferred by Fox (such as not bearing arms, and being simply dressed; Perrot and Rich were notoriously snappy dressers) mattered not a jot for Rich: "whether all these things may not be rational and useful in the Kingdom of Nature without sin?" Calling God to witness was for Rich an example of Fox and Richard Hubberthorne's hypocrisy.[16] Rich's unguarded use of biblical figures landed him in trouble when, in disposing a financial gift on the Calvert family, he unfortunately called Giles Calvert (the great radical publisher) "that Harlot who (in his time and day) so kindly and readily did receive the New Light."[17] His opponents immediately proclaimed that he had called Mrs Calvert a whore. In Rich's view, Nayler was hounded by Fox as well as persecuted by the magistrates: Nayler's silence in front of Fox an honest attempt to rise above his predicament in the terms of the spirit he professed. Fox's offering of his foot for Nayler to kiss (having first offered his hand, although this was not how Fox related the episode[18]) was a nasty display of power on Fox's part. For Rich, Fox was a dissimulator whose dangerous presence had been divinely predicted. He writes:

> I met *G.F.* and went to see him where he lodged; with great moderation he spake to me, of many things I found him wise as an Angel of Light, and as one that had all knowledge, and understood all mysteries. After this he sent for me privately alone, where (abiding in my simplicity and integrity) I saw that God had chosen the foolish things to confound the wise: And then it was given me, that G.F. is the star fallen from Heaven, to whom was given the key of the bottomless pit, and was King of the Locusts that came out of the smoak thereof, (which Bramble the Trees have chosen for their King) whose name and nature is to destroy. The consideration of which, moves me to acquaint thee of a Dream I had in the year 1655. Whilst I was a Prisoner in *Banbury*, I thought I was hunting the Fox with Hounds (a sport I much affected in my youth) and that the Fox ran into a great City, where we were at a loss. My self searching and hollowing in my sleep, and a Dog (blood red, I thought) run following the Fox out of the Town; at which I awoke, and told this my dream to my fellow prisoners.[19]

Rich became a universalist and practiced Christian charity by distributing funds lavishly to churches and sects of various persuasions (including the Quakers), notably in the aftermath of the Great Fire of London. His emphasis upon a general redemption and charity makes him resemble in some respects the Leveller William Walwyn. Both shared an interest in the literature of Pyrrhonic scepticism (especially Montaigne and Charron), and both used scepticism to justify a radical religious position.[20] But Walwyn apparently had no time for the kind of heady, mystical literature that intrigued Rich and sustained many other religious radicals.[21] For Rich, Thomas à Kempis's *Imitatio Christi,* Nicholas of Cusa's *De Idiota* and Benet of Canfield's *Rule of Perfection* (which he mistakenly thought was by Cusa), were "written by a Divine Spirit, and [I] do recommend them to all that are partakers of the Divine Nature."[22] Then a whole series of orthodox Catholic devotional manuals (by Caussin, Walter Montague, J.V. Canes, and Thomas Vane) are recommended as by "Wise Men, lovers of Wisdom, and well worth the reading by Men of Knowledg and Understanding." More controversial Catholic works he read to "treasure up in *Joseph's* Storehouse" what came from the Holy Spirit, and to discard all else. In line with Rich's typically enthusiastic reading of the Bible as a spiritual allegory, the Roman Catholic concept of purgatory was redefined as a form of meditative self-denial, before the believer enters blessedness. It is indeed the "purgation" stage set out in mystical works like the *Theologica Germanica.*[23] Further books, from the *Table* of Cebes (understood as an ancient Greek prefiguration of Christian perfection) and Epictetus (elsewhere the favourite reading of the notoriously irreligious republican Henry Marten) to the writings of Sir Henry Vane, add up to form the profile of a deeply meditative set of seeking perfectionists, who felt no need for any reliance upon a visible church, and who sought to live by their inward vision of an intensely felt new dispensation of love.[24] Yet though Rich, like Nayler, had not compromised while Fox was seeking some form of accommodation with the Protectorate in the mid-1650s, there is little doubt that Rich and his Church of the First Born also compromised during the Restoration years, replacing extravagant gesture with bookish introspection, and the exit to the West Indies is evidence of a retreat from the unyielding ground of religious controversy in England.

In fact, everyone compromised. With the exception of the Fifth Monarchist risings of the early 1660s, and the sporadic and nebulous evidence provided by Professor Greaves' study,[25] most radicals effectively achieved some form of accommodation with the new regime or they adapted to the changed circumstances of the Restoration. But then again, most of the extreme radicals had been compromising in some sense since 1650. Christopher Hill sees the process as part of what he has called the "experience of defeat." The Quakers were especially prominent in this pattern, but not in any obvious sense. Fox's *Journal* is difficult to rely on for evidence about the moments in time it recounts.[26]

Nonetheless, Fox and his circle seem to have been attempting to persuade the Protectorate government that Quakers were no great threat to the public order of the Commonwealth. Fox's encounters with Cromwell, insofar as they are reliable, reveal an affinity of piety between the two men. Their common ground is symptomatic of the ground of negotiation between Quakers themselves, as they emerged from various different positions in the early 1640s. There were of course platforms upon which the early Quakers based their appeal, and these had stylistic manifestations, some of which have become the object of study in current scholarship. But one does not have to stray very far from the "central ground" (but I hesitate even to use that phrase) of the early Friends to find difference and negotiation. It is this sense of difference which is so important in that it was instrumental in the definitions of different states of being among the early Friends. And while the Quaker movement was establishing a discipline and more clearly defined set of central beliefs in the 1660s and 1670s, Rich was celebrating diversity of belief as evidence of the power of the Spirit: "God teacheth and leadeth his people diversly, now after this manner, and another after another manner; also that there are diversity of Gifts, different Adminstrations and Operations, but all wrought by one and the same Spirit."[27]

In an influential article on Quaker prose style, Jackson I. Cope has seen these differences as in part a consequence of social and status difference.[28] The Friends found their early followers among the educated and the gentry (even a few of the nobility), as well as the lower orders. The habits of lawyers, for instance, produced a different kind of register from the programmatic pamphlets of Burrough, Farnworth, Hubberthorne and Nayler. Respectable, well-educated and elevated Friends also wrote closer to the claims of their religion in private correspondence than they did in printed, publicly circulated works.

But there is also a sense in which the differences were a function of a certain kind of misunderstanding. It is not at all clear that the early Friends understood each other even to the degree experienced by the other sects. A religion founded upon largely irrational and intuitive impulses is likely to experience difficulties when in the process of forming itself, and when understanding the meaning of its beliefs. The early letter exchanges, and the early disagreements, are at least as much a matter of emergent differences of position (and of strugglings to reach mutual comprehension) as they are battles for authority. What Friends found themselves saying in interrogations and trials bears the mark of spontaneity as well as planned defence: their inquisitors forced them to articulate their witness in hitherto unforeseen ways. By the early 1650s, the enthusiastic diaspora from which the Quakers emerged had moved sufficiently far from the habits of orthodox Protestantism for there to be little recognizable inherited framework to work with. At the same time, the speed and the widespread nature of the Friends' emergence further accentuated these areas of uncertainty between individuals, beyond the basic acceptance of the primacy of the light within. For many of these early Friends and neo-Quakers (such as Rice Jones of Nottingham, with whom Fox was associated in the "Children of the Light," just before the Quakers emerged properly), we have very little or no evidence of their thought, behavior or expression.

By contrast, the Muggletonians had a very definite set of beliefs, extending from a model of faith and sect discipline to an entire view of the cosmos, as well as a tight network of connections based upon well-regulated codes of letter-writing.[29]

It is not at all clear that the early Friends always understood each other, or even understood the concepts they were using themselves. To Fox can be attributed certain positions with regard, for instance, to ideas of divine immanence, but to do so necessarily means attaching a fixed position to him. Sometimes, this amounts to an anachronistic invention from a twentieth-century perspective, and sometimes a submission to an understanding of Fox as his opponents among the Independents and Baptists would have seen him. The relative lack of precise doctrinal definition in Fox's own writing in the epistles of the 1650s (practically none of his preached sermons survive) must be in part due to the fact that he had simply not worked out where he stood particularly clearly on certain issues. It is notable that although Fox, like Rich, collected books from the *Spiritualisten* tradition, he did not show them in his own writing in the way that Rich did, and in the bizarre way that other artisanal prophets, like Thomas Tany, seem to have done.[30] Did he read them at all? To this extent, the early Quakers represent an abrupt break with the tradition, and its habits, from which they emerged. Fox's haziness is compounded in the *Journal* not only by a retreat from earlier enthusiasm (or enthusiastic behavior), but also by a pervasive habit of writing in deliberately simplistic terms on theological issues. The lesson learned of successful proselytization was that simplicity was a tool far stronger than definition.

But at the same time, there is little doubt that between them, the early Quakers centered around Fox did gradually come to have a censorious impact, as they transformed their movement from a sect into a church. The account of the questioning of John Perrot by Fox, Isaac Penington and others has the uneasy and threatening feeling of an interrogation. Nayler did not live into the new era, but Perrot, Rich and others took enthusiasm into a realm where we might have expected other early Friends to have gone, had they not submitted to weekly, monthly and quarterly meetings. Rich's gestural, spiritual and intellectual openness was in a sense more in keeping with the spirit of early 1650s Quakerism than the more restrictive Quaker practices of the Restoration.

And perhaps to discard bookishness further encouraged a forgetting of disagreements and differences. On the level of the dynamics of interaction within the Friends, this meant the form of silent meeting and then discussion in which a singular view would be reached intuitively, waiting upon the Lord, without dispute; a mode of procedure that outsiders usually found very difficult to grasp or accept. In this light, Fox's authoritarianism in the eyes of the enthusiasts was simply regarded as that of *primus inter pares* by the orthodox Quakers. They did not think of themselves as authoritarian in any sense. The meetings, first day, quarterly, men's and women's, all ministered the authority of the light in a just and appropriate way.

On the other hand, and certainly during the 1650s, there were several areas in which differences of definition and comprehension were bound to occur and which at the same time could not be suppressed because their expression was at the very heart of what it was to be a sectarian. The first is traditionally known as the expression of heresy, and in the case of the mid-century radicals was to do with the definition of the body. The relationship between the body and the soul, between matter and substance, was one of the foundations of sectarian definition, intellectually, as an article of faith and as a force in the formation of particular groups. Mortalism (the belief that in some sense or other the soul remains with the body after death until the general resurrection) marks off many of the more extreme radical religious positions (from the General Baptists to the most extreme individual prophets), despite the fact that many Anglican clergymen during the following century became mortalists.[31] Similarly, the entire Muggletonian organization depended upon the acceptance among believers of a complete cosmology. The same appears to be true of the prophet Thomas Tany.

While the opacity of much Quaker writing appears to belie any such interest – or if they had such an interest, they hid it – very early Quaker writing, along with Seekers and Ranters, and the rest of the milieu, is interested in these things. The recent case made for Fox's development of a doctrine of "Christopresentism," if not of any statement of the possibility that the inner light makes the flesh holy may be an exaggeration, or the result of a too willing ear given to Fox's opponents among the Puritan ministers, but the fact is that such concerns are important.[32] With regard to the matter of writing, the question is of how the body is *figured*.

While the less enthusiastic Quakers claimed that they believed in the literal truth of the Scriptures, as a history of real historical events, and as a key to the light within, the enthusiasts stressed the scripture solely as an interior allegory, as a record of the workings of the inner light within individuals. We must also acknowledge that the early Quakers often assumed that the body underwent a change when it was inhabited by the inner light, that is, by the substance of Christ:

> Is not he that denyes Jesus to be come in the flesh an Antichrist? Then *Edward Reyner* hath no wrong done him to be called Antichrist: for He denyes the Substance of the Deity to be communicable. Is not Christ Jesus of the Substance of the Deity? Is it not said, *Christ in you the Hope of Glory?*[33]

Thus, scriptural language as allegory of inner light actually becomes a kind of anatomy for the regenerate Quaker. This would explain the hermetic, occult and physiological reading indulged in by Perrot and Rich.

Other radicals assumed that the glorified body was in some sense a superior version of the human form: Thomas Tany, rather like the occultist Van Helmont, believed that the soul was a kind of crystal man. The Quaker perfected body is not skeletal or "formal" but textual, fragmented many times over, and dispersed. Another Quaker heretic defended by Robert Rich, John Penneyman, used terms very similar to Perrot's when addressing Fox:

> The Mountain-Stone hath broke Thy Toes,
> Thy Vitals now must feel its Blows.
> May skilful Archers every Hour
> Shoot Truth's Arrows from their Tower,
> Against thy persecuting Power.[34]

In this light, of course, what is usually seen as merely metaphorical becomes something much more challenging: a real transformation. For Rich, the Spirit was explicitly heavenly flesh that came to live inside each person, so that everyone who has the inner light has two bodies.[35] Fox persistently argued with disputants that all forms of "light" were not merely natural, but Rich has gone beyond this to a fully fledged picture of human interiority as celestial flesh, a literal section of the Godhead: "he which sanctifieth and those that are sanctified are all one and the same pure substance."[36] And when Perrot talks about the soul as female – "Wisdom is my mother and Counsel are her breasts. I am a child and desire ever to be found a sucker of the substance thereof" – he may well be assuming a much more thoroughgoing transformation than we have hitherto supposed. Rich lived in this world and took it at the Restoration, unlike Fox, Burrough, Hubberthorne and Farnworth, into a realm of extremely abstract, highly optimistic speculation, although the evidence does not tell us to what extent the old practices of the Naylerites survived after 1660. By publishing some of Nayler's correspondence, Rich certainly intended to keep Nayler's voice of the 1650s alive.

The stress on at least the spiritual equality of men and women by Quakers, and the prominent role played by Quaker women as authors, meant that discourse was given the presence of a distinctive style(s) by Quaker women. Yet this is not merely a matter of attitudes towards prophecy, but also something that facilitated the expression of new aspects of gender difference. Friends effectively expressed their consociation in a language of mutual interpenetration that operates in terms of a fusing of the (represented) human body. Again, Rich was at the forefront here, for by assuming the name of Mordecai, he was identifying Nayler as Esther, since Mordecai was Esther's cousin and retainer in her eponymous book in the Old Testament.

Another crucially vital area was the relationship between word and wealth, or at least well-being. The most far-sighted religious and economic writing of the period must be Gerard Winstanley's theories of a return to paradise through the common cultivation of common land, in a holy revolt against enclosure. To justify his theory he had to redefine the distinction between man, God and nature, and it was this that provided the limits as well as the possibilities in his project. By the same token, and on a rather more sophisticated level, James Harrington found that he had to redescribe property and political relations through complex analogies with anatomy and astronomy in order to arrive at his model of an English republic. In a way, Quaker writing is no different. Fox continually makes the point that Friends were committed to acts of charity, and he is concerned to demonstrate his own financial sufficiency during his travels. In fact, Quaker style slowly takes on board monied respectability as it mediates between great sympathy for poverty (especially due to the exactions from tithes) and the extremes of aggressive mercantilism and plantation (witness Fox's attempts to modulate the attitudes of slave-owning Friends in America). Rich freely gave his money away (he could afford to), while Fox complained of Perrot's expenses while on his mission in the Mediterranean.

The control manifested in orthodox Quaker expression in part accounts for the extraordinary success of the Friends, even in their early days, for their words and their silent worship embodied the transformed subjectivity of radical Puritanism while not dismantling the property relations in which many radicals were fixed. On the other hand, their writing stood against the socio-spiritual abuses (tithes, and so on) that many radicals did protest against.

All of these areas relate back to the debate at the heart of all attitudes towards "truth" within Puritanism, the location and meaning of God's Word, and specifically its relationship with human language. A recent approach, informed by psychoanalytic theory, supposes that the Quakers pursued an absolute escape from forms: Bunyan's immersion in allegory (in which repressed culture returns) and Protestant scripturalism are kinds of enculturement identified by Quakers as "forms."[37] If this is the case, the question begged is what is the nature of the inner light that moves inside Quakers and their words? Since the answer is that godly language only ever reveals itself as an allegory of the internal working of the inner light, Quaker language has, as we have already seen, effectively become an *anatomy* of Quaker regeneration. Most early Quakers understood this, but the enthusiasts, Nayler and Rich foremost among them, recognized this in the most acute of ways. If Bunyan was true to his (radical) Protestantism in allowing the repressed to return in his allegories so that we see representations of his own material world describing godliness, for the Quakers, repression and its return was replaced by a complete transformation of the "language" one owned: into *scriptura rediviva*. This was as much to say that there was no "sinful" self to cast out, no carnal remnant that remained indelibly in place, despite the assurance of grace. Instead, the early Friends imagined that they had transformed their entire beings: they were prefallen Adams and Eves in a perfect natural world. In this sense, their daring verbal experimentation was the most absolute act of scriptural hermeneutics ever made. It also explains why Fox and the others were both so uncertain in their restatings of body and soul definitions, and why they spoke only in scriptural terms. The body has indeed become scripture in the Quaker imagination. Hence also the Quaker claim (which outraged most Puritan opponents) that the natural can embody the divine – since the natural is all we can ever have, including scripture language. The Quaker enthusiasts assumed the continuity of the Book of Scripture and the Book of Nature to a far greater degree than most of the orthodox Friends.

The truth about the early Quakers is that if we forget the full dimensions of their internal differences, their permeable borders with associated religious radicals, and the impact of their defences against opponents, we miss very large elements of the complete picture. The rhythms, incantations and naming concerns identified by Cope are indelible marks of their identity, but their struggles of self-understanding reveal a more diverse, penetrating and absorbing use of words and the body. It is now time for full-length studies of these issues that, given the mass of available evidence, can only be skirted in an article of this length.

NOTES

1. See, for instance, Christopher Hill, "Radical Prose in 17th-Century England: From Marprelate to the Levellers," *Essays in Criticism*, 32 (1982): 95–118; Nigel Smith, *Perfection Proclaimed: Language and Literature in English Radical Religion 1640-1660* (Oxford: Clarendon Press, 1989); Thomas N. Corns, *Uncloistered Virtue: English Political Literature 1640–1660* (Oxford: Clarendon Press, 1992), ch.5; four essays in James Holstun, ed., *Pamphlet Wars: Prose in the English Revolution* (London: Cass, 1992), 14–44, 60–75, 112–33, 158–204.

2. See Timothy Kenyon, *Utopian Communism and Political Thought in Early Modern England* (London: Pinter Press, 1989), Pt.III; see also the corrective argument in J.C. Davis, "Formal Utopia/Informal Millennium: The Struggle between Form and Substance as a Context for Seventeenth-Century Utopianism," in K. Kumar and S. Bann, eds., *Utopias and the Millennium* (London: Reaktion Books, 1993), 17–45.

3. Jacques Derrida, "The Law of Genre," *Critical Inquiry:* 1 (1980): 55–81.

4. Smith, *Perfection Proclaimed*, Pt.I.

5. See Nigel Smith, *Literature and Revolution in England, 1640–1660* (New Haven and

London: Yale University Press, 1994), chs.1, 2, 4, 6, 9; Joad Raymond, ed., *Making the News: An Anthology of the Newsbooks of Revolutionary England, 1641-1660* (Moreton-in-Marsh: The Windrush Press, 1993), Introduction; Sharon Achinstein, *Milton and the Revolutionary Reader* (Princeton: Princeton University Press, 1994).

6. See above, Kate Peters, "Patterns of Quaker Authorship, 1652–56."
7. "Exporting Enthusiasm: John Perrot and the Quaker Epic," in Thomas Healy and Jonathan Sawday, edd., *Literature and the English Civil War* (Cambridge, 1990), 248–64; see also Nigel Smith, *Literature and Revolution*, 225–6.
8. James Holstun, review of T. Healy and J. Sawday, edd., *Literature and the English Civil War* (Cambridge, 1990) in *JEGP* 92 (1993): 129–31.
9. Anon., *The Grand Imposter Examined* (London, 1657), 21.
10. Ibid., 23.
11. G.F. Nuttall, "The Last of James Nayler, Robert Rich and the Church of the First Born," *Friends Quarterly* 60 (1985): 527–34.
12. For Bacon, see Nuttall, op. cit.
13. Robert Rich, *Epistles* (London, 1680), Sig. A3v. On the politics of "forms," see J.C. Davis, op. cit.
14. Robert Rich, *A Testimony to the Truth*, 4–5.
15. Robert Rich, *Mr Robert Rich His Second Letters from Barbados* (London, 1679), 6.
16. Ibid., 26, 34–5.
17. Robert Rich, *Love Without Dissimulation* (London, 1666), 7. The phrase is meant allegorically of course.
18. George Fox, *Journal*, ed. N. Smith (Harmondsworth: Penguin Books, forthcoming).
19. Robert Rich, *Mr Robert Rich His Second Letters from Barbados* (London, 1679), 41–2.
20. See N. Smith, "The Charge of Atheism and the Language of Radical Speculation 1640-1660," in Michael Hunter and David Wootton, eds., *Atheism in Early Modern Europe* (Oxford: Clarendon Press, 1992), 111–30.
21. See Smith, *Perfection Proclaimed*, Pt. II.
22. *Epistles*, 11.
23. *Mr Robert Rich his Second Letters*, 24.
24. See also the even more extravagant list in Robert Rich, *Love Without Dissimulation* (London, 1666), 6–7.
25. Richard Greaves, *Deliver Us from Evil: The Radical Underground in Britain, 1660–1663* (New York and Oxford: Oxford University Press, 1986).
26. See below, Thomas N. Corns, "'No Man's Copy': The Critical Problem of Fox's *Journal*."
27. Robert Rich, *A Testimony to the Truth* (1679), 1.
28. Jackson I. Cope, "Seventeenth-Century Quaker Style," *PMLA*: 71 (1956): 725–54.
29. C. Hill, B. Reay and W.M. Lamont, *The World of the Muggletonians* (London: Yemple Smith: 1983).
30. J.L. Nickalls, "George Fox's Library," *JFHS*: 28 (1931): 3–21; I am grateful to Ariel Hessayon for letting me see his very original work on Tany.
31. N.T. Burns, *Christian Mortalism from Tyndale to Milton* (Camb., Mass.: Harvard University Press, 1972); B.W. Young, "'The Soul-Sleeping System': Politics and Heresy in Eighteenth-Century England," *JEH* 45 (1994): 64–81.
32. Richard G. Bailey, *New Light on George Fox and Early Quakerism: The Making and Unmaking of a God* (San Francisco: Mellen Research University Press, 1992).
33. Martin Mason, *The Proud Pharisee Reproved* (London, 1655), 36.
34. [John Penneyman], "Phil. Ang.," *A Bright Shining Light* (London, 1680), 8.
35. Robert Rich, *A Testimony of the Truth*, 2–3. Rich's argument confused opponents, who also saw Mariolatry in his notion of the Virgin Birth.
36. Ibid., 8.
37. Thomas H. Luxon, "'Other Mens Words' and 'New Birth': Bunyan's Antihermeneutics of Experience," *TSLL* 36 (1994): 258–90.

From Seeker to Finder: The Singular Experiences of Mary Penington

NORMAN T. BURNS

A notable feature of Oliver Cromwell's letter of 25 October 1646 to his daughter Bridget Ireton is the cheerful spirit in which he reports to Bridget the mental distress of her sister Elizabeth Claypole, only seventeen and not yet a year married:

> your Sister Claypole is (I trust in mercy) exercised with some perplexed thoughts. She sees her own vanity and carnal mind, bewailing it: she seeks after (as I hope also) that which will satisfy. And thus to be a seeker is to be of the best sect next to a finder; and such an one shall every faithful humble seeker be at the end. Happy seeker, happy finder! Who ever tasted that the Lord is gracious, without some sense of self, vanity, and badness? Who ever tasted that graciousness of His, and could go [become] less in desire, and less than pressing after full enjoyment?[1]

Why is this father not distressed that his favorite daughter is distressed? Optimism about the situation is implicit in the scriptural verses that Cromwell's writing "she seeks" may have recalled to him: those verses in Luke in which Jesus promises that the Father will "give the Holy Spirit to them that ask him" (11:13) and that one had only to "seek, and ye shall find" (11:9). Moreover, the thought that his beloved daughter is perplexed and bewails her own nature cheers Cromwell because he is committed to the idea that introspection rigorously conducted is the surest way to the joy of being fully open to God's grace, letting Christ into the heart, "that which will satisfy."[2] This idea is hardly unusual, some sense of it being shared right across the Interregnum religious spectrum from Presbyterian to Quaker. But when radical spiritualists greatly magnified the direct operations of divine grace on the human heart by slighting the role of church ordinances and the preaching of the paid clergy as conduits of grace, this idea of an unmediated relationship between the believer and Christ divided churchman and "enthusiast." As we shall see, a considerable number of devout people (often called "Seekers" came to disdain all formal worship in churches even before they were able to find satisfaction in private worship; their seeking could be more prolonged, more uncertain, and thus more painful than Cromwell here appears to think.

We know little more than this letter tells us about the spiritual life of Elizabeth Claypole. It may be that she never experienced very intensely the states her father described, either the perplexities of seeking with its vexatious discontent with the self, or the delights of finding the "full enjoyment" of "that which satisfies." But the spiritual journey that Cromwell proposed for his daughter was taken in some fashion by many in mid-seventeenth-century England. About the time that Cromwell discussed Lady Claypole's spiritual state, another woman of property, Lady Mary Proud Springett, a widow of twenty-one and mother of two small children, was in the deepest confusion about her spiritual condition. Her desolation was so great that she reached a state not anticipated in Cromwell's scheme. Some twenty years later, when she wrote about that crisis in her engaging autobiography *Experiences in the Life of Mary Penington (Written by Herself)*, she declares that she had taken up vain and carnal activities *because* she had tried so hard to seek the Lord:

> In this restless state I entertained every sort of notion that arose in that day . . .; but still sorrow and trouble was the end of all, and I began to conclude that the Lord and his truth was, but that it was not made known to any upon earth; and I determined no more to enquire after Him or it, for it was in vain to seek Him, being not to be found. For some time, . . . I thought nothing about religion, but . . . ran into many excesses and vanities; as foolish mirth, carding, dancing, singing, and frequenting of music meetings; . . . gratifying the lust of the eye, the lust of the flesh, and the pride of life. . . . But in the midst of all this my heart was constantly sad, and pained beyond expression. . . .
>
> To all this excess and folly I was not hurried by being captivated with such things, but sought in them relief from the discontent of my mind; not having found what I sought after, and longed for, in the practice of religious duties. I would often say to myself, What is all this to me? . . . I do these things because I am weary, and know not what else to do: it is not my delight, it hath not power over me. I had rather serve the Lord, if I knew how acceptably.[3]

Penington's statement inverts the received wisdom about the interplay of worldliness and religion. The common understanding, then as now, was that churchgoing or other forms of religious devotion lead one away from the follies and vanities of the world, that Christian devotion brings comfort to the troubled heart. That is the basis of Cromwell's optimism for Lady Elizabeth: seekers find. It is precisely because Penington had zealously practiced her religious duties and sought comfort in "every sort of notion that arose in that day"[4] that she suffers such mental distress and in her disappointment seeks relief in "many excesses and vanities." Cromwell thinks that Lady Elizabeth's bewailing her vanities and carnal mind will help her press after full enjoyment of God, whereas Lady Mary bewails the emptiness of the available ways of Christian worship, concludes that it is vain to seek the Lord, and her resultant sorrow moves her into a joyless pursuit of worldly pleasures.

Mary Penington left in her *Experiences* the history of her interior life, a record of how she got into this desperate condition, and how she emerged from it: "a true, though brief account, of many passages from my childhood to the time it was written. . . . for the use of my children, and some few particular friends" (*EMP*, 48). The book is valuable for its affecting evocation of a spiritual life lived in inviolable privacy even in the midst of a loving family, a life that could yet fully engage with "the world" when its demands did not interfere with religion. Penington's life shows how inward-looking Puritan piety could lead to a growing dissatisfaction with the "duties" defined by organized congregations until the zealous churchmember by degrees becomes a Seeker. Penington gives an intimate account of the states of mind that were such excellent seed-ground for the Quaker message when the movement swept through England.[5] It will be useful to preface this discussion with a sketch of that life.

The title narrative of *Experiences in the Life of Mary Penington (Written by Herself)* is Mary Springett Penington's account of her spiritual journey from her childhood into her age and final illness. She was born about 1625, the only child of Sir John Proud and Anne Fagge of Kent, who left her an orphaned heiress at the age of three.[6] She tells of a rebellious Puritan childhood (from about age nine) in the household of her guardian, Sir Edward Partridge (who generally conformed to the Church of England), together with his widowed sister Madam Springett and her three children, one of whom was William. After some years at Cambridge and the Inns of Court, the now Sir William returned home and, about January 1642, he and Mary were married "refusing the use of a ring'; he was twenty and she perhaps not yet seventeen. She describes their rigorous repudiation of many of the "dead forms" of the established church, William's early death in February 1644, and the posthumous birth of Gulielma (who was to be the wife of William Penn), named after her father. Then began Mary's years of spiritual dissatisfaction, "being wearied in seeking and not finding" (*EMP*, 38). She rejected all church ways although she had no satisfactory private worship to replace them. After ten years in this condition she married Isaac Penington Jr. By 1659, when she was about 34 years old, Mary and Isaac Penington were practicing Quakers.[7] This part of the manuscript, from her girlhood through her "convincement" (*EMP*, 17–48), was completed some "considerable time" before Penington in 1668 thought it worth leaving with a friend who would, after the author's death, "show it to such as had a love for me" (*EMP*, 47–8); Penington did not go through with that plan, but from 1676 to the end of June 1682 (about three months before her death), she added to the manuscript from time to time – accounts of the Peningtons' sufferings at the hands of the law, of house building, of her persistent illnesses, and of her attempts to disencumber herself of outward concerns as she prepares for death.

Together with the *Experiences* Norman Penney edited "A Letter from Mary Penington to her Grandson, Springet Penn," a splendid narrative of the life and death of Sir William Springett that abounds with anecdotes that elucidate the character of the boy's grandfather. Penington wrote the account in 1680, the year in which she made her will, apparently as part of her program to settle the things that were necessary to be done before she died. Although her grandson Springett was but five years old at the time of writing, Penington wanted to be sure that when the boy grew up he fully appreciated the nobility of his grandfather's character. "A Letter" has many merits in its own right, but in this essay I shall use it only to suggest that Penington's sense of genre led her to employ in it a style very different from the one she used in most of the *Experiences*.

Penington's *Experiences* is an unusual autobiography because, in the main, it neglects external events, mentioning them only insofar as they bear upon her "experiences" – those spiritual states of mind and feeling that alone engage her and seem to her worth setting down. She emphasizes the concerns, anxieties, and bewilderments of her spiritual life as she struggles, without apparent confidants or guides, to leave behind the empty forms of conventional worship and find on her own a mode of worship that could satisfy her craving for an unmediated relationship with God, for a glimpse of the "exchanges of glory in the Saint" that John Saltmarsh thought characterized life in the spirit.[8]

Mary Penington never seems merely to "fall away" from regular worship services. Rather, she moves away from them energetically, without hesitation or uncertainty. There can be no going back, even when she can see no way forward. When she reaches the nadir of her journey and takes up with vain, worldly people, Penington does not present her action as a weakness, but as a moral choice. She has participated fully in the life of religious duties in churches and is sure that anyone who claims that that life is comforting is false, thus certainly worse than her new profane companions. Her giving up church participation, she explains, is principled, though church members of course consider it a weakness, evidence of "a loose mind":

I gave over all manner of religious exercises in my family and in private, with much grief, for my delight was in being exercised about religion. I left not those things in a loose mind, as some judged that kept in them; for had I found I performed thereby what the Lord required of me, . . . I could gladly have continued in the practice of them; I being zealously affected about the several things that were accounted duties; a zealous Sabbath-keeper, and fasting often; praying in private, rarely less than three times a day, many times oftener; a hearer of sermons on all occasions, both lectures, fasts and thanksgiving. . . .Oh! this was not parted with but because I found it polluted, and my rest must not be there.

I now had my conversation among a people that had no religion, being ashamed to be thought religious, . . . not finding my heart with the appearance. . . . I . . . thought the professors of every sort worse than the profane, they boasted so much of what I knew they had not attained to; I having been zealous in all things which they pretended to, and could not find the purging of the heart, or answer of acceptation from the Lord. (*EMP,* 28–30)

Penington's disgust with the existing Christian congregations is understandable when one considers that Interregnum religious discussion featured doctrinal and organizational issues, all of them endlessly and usually acrimoniously disputed among the churches and sects. Creeds were propounded, heresies were denounced, schemes of organization advocated; there was little agreement, but all parties claimed that their positions were essential to true religion and best conformed to the divine will. For many Christians it was not clear how these hard words advanced their personal devotions or the reform of the heart, but their concerns tended to be lost in the din of public controversy.

Mary Penington and many other devout people found this state of religious affairs utterly unsatisfying. With so many opinions in contention, what church or teacher could speak with authority? What beliefs were necessary to salvation, and how was one to worship God rightly? How could one be sure about these matters? Such questions were central in a culture aspiring to live by a purely apostolic faith and practice, but many Christians thought their religious institutions gave unsatisfactory guidance in matters that were urgently in need of clarification and certainty. These disaffected people issued no creeds and established no polities, but drifted away from the churches and sects, or maintained but the loosest of ties with them, open to preachers like George Fox who could "speak to their condition" and call them out of the churches.

Mary Penington's memoir, I believe, splendidly represents the mood of these disaffected people, the kind of people Fox had in mind when in 1647 he "saw the harvest white, and the Seed of God lying thick in the ground, as ever did wheat that was sown outwardly, and none to gather it."⁹ They were often called, by themselves and others, "Seekers." Whether Seekers formed a new sect themselves is unclear, but many people, like Mary Penington, must have developed Seeker attitudes without joining together, not even in informal groups. As William Penn describes the Seekers in his preface to Fox's *Journal*, it is not easy to say whether he thinks they are a sect or a mood; he writes about people who "left all visible churches and societies and wandered up and down as sheep without a shepherd, and as doves without their mates; *seeking* their beloved, but could not find Him (as their souls desired to know Him), whom their souls loved above their chiefest joy. These persons were called Seekers by some and the Family of Love by others."¹⁰ In the years following the death of her husband, Penington's mood closely paralleled that of Penn's sad Seekers. When she had a dream appearing to have religious significance, she made nothing of it, "believing there was nothing manifest since the apostles' days, that was true religion; for I knew nothing to be so certainly of God, that I could shed my blood in the defence of it" (*EMP*, 32–3). She too had abandoned all worship and religious duties. "I thought the beloved of my soul was neither night nor day, with me," she writes. When her mood turned tender or tearful, she attributed it to planetary influence rather than to the influence of God's spirit on her heart; she was not satisfied, however, for "I was like the parched heath, and the hunted hart for water, so great was my thirst after that which I did not believe was near me" (*EMP*, 34–5).

There was another sort of Seeker who expected the Holy Spirit to show that a church or "dispensation" had divine authority by some external sign, often a charismatic Apostle figure who appeared to be authorized by special prophetic powers, possibly including the miraculous. Laurence Clarkson's autobiography, *The Lost Sheep Found*, shows us the exemplar of this type of Seeker: in a journey across three decades Clarkson narrates his movement from his native Church of England successively to the Presbyterians, Independents, Antinomians, Baptists, Seekers, and Ranters until this lost sheep was found by the uniquely authoritative John Reeve, to whom God spoke as he had previously to Moses and Paul, "audibly to the hearing of the ear."¹¹ Clarkson's pilgrimage is marked by his confident, self-assured tone, with few indications that he felt the distress that might afflict one who had not yet found a satisfying relationship with God. Clarkson names the preachers and sectarian leaders he met, the officers who examined and imprisoned him, and the women he was adulterous with; he names the churches and sects he took up with, commenting on their doctrines and their effect on his developing thought. This sheep, whether lost or found, seems never to have had a purely introspective, or even a quiet, moment.

Mary Penington's autobiography is wholly different, in style as well as substance. In her *Experiences* she shows no interest in authority nor, indeed, in people or places. In his astute essay on the prose style of the early Quakers, Jackson Cope observes that early Quakers characteristically were not concerned with the particularity of external experience; in Fox's *Journal*, for example,

> The physical scene is not England, but the image of his spiritual struggle. . . . Again, it is not that the night is lacking in reality, it is that reality for long stretches of the narrative seems to consist only in Fox, and in the sweep of day and darkness; and that the day and darkness of the journey seem so irresistibly to mirror the spiritual state of Fox, that they become charged with spiritual content.[12]

When Penington describes her "experiences" as a Seeker, external circumstances are even more neglected. She names no one whom she associated with, nor any church or sect she may have encountered. She says nothing of her only son by William, who must have died during this time. Despite the fact that she reared Gulielma alone in the ten years of her widowhood and that she entrusted the manuscript of *Experiences* to Gulielma's care (*EMP*, 17), Penington mentions her daughter only to say that she refused to have her baptized. She says nothing of where she lived, or in whose company, during this difficult time.[13]

Even when she describes her two years with her husband William Springett, there is no sense of a situation in which there is interchange between two devout people trying to find their way in spiritual matters for which there is no sufficient external guide; they seem instead to think and act in unison. She does not give a single distinguishing feature to William, who is made even more indistinct by the fact that she does not state his name, here or anywhere in the memoir:

> We scrupled many things then in use amongst those accounted honest people, viz.: singing David's Psalms in metre. We tore out of our Bibles the common prayer, and also the singing psalms, as being the inventions of vain poets, not being written for that use. . . . We were also brought off from the use of bread and wine, and water baptism. We looked into the Independent way, but saw death there, and that there was not the thing our souls sought after.
>
> In this state my dear husband died, hoping in the promises afar off, not seeing or knowing Him that is invisible to be so near him;

and that it was He that showed unto him his thoughts, and made manifest the good and the evil. (*EMP,* 26–7)

The key to why the relationship is show in such a way is in the final two clauses. At the time William's knowledge of the operations of God with his people was not sufficient for him to recognize that it was God who brought his ideas to his consciousness and enabled him to discriminate between the good and the bad. It is God's grace operating in the individual heart that is illuminating, not the discourse even of inspired humans. Mary's understanding of this matter was in those days probably no better than her husband's, but in her maturity the now Quaker writer could explain it. All the blame is man's; all the good is God's. Mary Penington's narrative, like her type of seeking, is so unlike Clarkson's that it might be seen as a different genre. What affects her is not what people say or do, but what she learns when she is alone and able to open her heart to the operations of God's grace.

The figure of Penington in the *Experiences* is isolated. Even before her crisis in the years after she was widowed, she knew few who felt the way she did and none who could assist her in finding what she sought, "the purging of the heart, or answer of acceptance from the Lord." Even her "dear husband" William, as we have seen, and her "dear husband" Isaac, as we shall see, get little attention in the narrative, presumably because they have no role in her private struggles. Penington doubtless loved and admired both husbands, but at all times in her narrative she holds her own spiritual nature aloof from them as from all others. It is instructive to see how her view of herself so sharply contrasts with that presented by another Parliamentary widow and memoirist, Lucy Hutchinson, who at about the same time told her children about their father and herself. Although Hutchinson too is a bold and heterodox Puritan spirit, she accords her beloved husband a role in fashioning her character that had no place in Penington's view of the formation of the self. Writing of herself in the third person, Hutchinson credits her husband John with extraordinary influence: "If he esteem'd her att a higher rate than she in her selfe could have deserv'd, he was the author of that vertue he doted on, while she only reflected his owne glories upon him: all that she was, with him, while he was here, and all that she is now at best is but his pale shade."[14] How distant this is from Penington's account of the moral process after she accepted the Quaker way! She blamed herself for disliking some Friends, but

after a time of deep secret sorrow, the Lord removed the wrong thing from me, blessing me with a large portion of his light, and the love and acceptance of his beloved ones. And He hath many times refreshed my soul in his presence, and given me assurance that I knew that estate in which He will never leave me nor suffer me to be drawn from all which He has graciously fulfilled. . . . I feel and know when I have slipped in word, deed, or thought; and also know where my help lieth, who is my advocate, and have recourse to Him who pardons and heals, and gives me to overcome. (*EMP*, 46–7)

Her "dear husband" Isaac is quite absent. There is no place for human figures in this spiritual landscape.

It is this presentation of herself as radically solitary as well as radically nonconforming that dominates Penington's narrative and leaves the impression of a courageous, strong-minded woman ready to suffer for what she believes in her heart. Her own radical Puritan behavior before her marriage to William and the youthful couple's casting off of "dead superstitions" during and after their wedding met with the disapproval of family and neighbors:

I regarded not their reproaches, that would say to me that no gentleman was of this way, and that I should marry some mean person or other. But they were disappointed, for the Lord touched the heart of him that was afterwards my husband, and my heart cleaved to him for the Lord's sake. . . . Though both very young, [we] were joined together in the Lord; refusing the use of a ring, and such like things then used, and not denied by any that we knew of. (*EMP*, 25–6)

On the evidence of her *Experiences* Penington did not need a husband to help her defy public opinion. By about age twelve, having privately discovered that rote or published prayer was entirely unsatisfactory, she withstood the reproofs and (worse, for a child) the ridicule of her guardians and the parish. She refused to join the priest in prayer at services, eventually would not hear the sermons of the parish priest and, in the face of "reasonings and threatenings," traveled to hear a suspended Puritan preacher instead. She would not join in family prayer and encouraged two maidservants to join her refusal, "at which the governors of the family were much disturbed, and made me the subject of their discourse in company, saying that I would pray with the spirit, and rejected godly men's prayers; that I was proud and schismatic; and that I went to those places to meet young men, and such like" (*EMP*, 23–4). Young Mary went on from strength to strength, drawing on seemingly inexhaustible inner resources. After William's death in 1644, when she was not yet twenty, Lady Mary refused to have Gulielma baptized at all.

It was an incomprehensible decision to people of her class as well as to her favorite Puritan clergymen. She faced down all the heavy artillery that could be brought against her: "I became a by-word and a hissing among the people of my own rank in the world; and a strange thing it was thought to be, among my relations and acquaintance; Such as were esteemed able ministers (and I formerly delighted to hear), were sent to persuade me; but I could not consent and be clear" (*EMP*, 28). Soon after, Penington moved through various church affiliations into her Seeker phase.

After ten years of widowhood and "seeking," Mary married Isaac Penington, apparently because she had finally found someone who felt the way she did though, to be sure, he seems to have been more in need of help than able to give spiritual assistance to his new wife:

> being wearied in seeking and not finding, I married my dear husband, Isaac Penington. My love was drawn toward him, because I found he saw the deceit of all nations, and lay as one that refused to be comforted by any appearance of religion, until He came to his temple, "who is truth and no lie." All things that appeared to be religion and were not so, were very manifest to him; so that, till then, he was sick and weary of all appearances. My heart became united to him, and I desired to be made serviceable to him in his disconsolate condition; for he was as one alone and miserable in this world. (*EMP*, 38–9)

Although Isaac is granted his name here, as William was not, Isaac too was pretty much a cipher in Mary's account of her spiritual struggle, which was shortly to climax with the coming of the Quakers into their life. Isaac's spiritual condition can hardly be distinguished from Mary's, at least as Mary presents it. One of her favorite words for her discouraged seeking is "weary." She is "weary of prayers" (*EMP*, 28) and "weary of doctrines" (*EMP*, 40), she indulges in worldly things "because I am weary" (*EMP*, 31), and she comes to this marriage "wearied in seeking and not finding," so when she tells us that Isaac was "weary of all appearances" of religion we see that the spiritual moods of two people are fused into one, just as the religious views of Mary and William Springett had been. In the pages that follow, which bring the Peningtons into Quakerism, we hear of Mary's solitary struggles, but nothing of the way in which Isaac came to be convinced. Perhaps that is as it should be since this is Mary's life, though we might justly expect that, since she has emphasized his "disconsolate condition," she will also say how he came out of it. But Mary has no sooner described Isaac's condition and stated her wish to be a companion to him than she immediately turns attention to her own inner state, which is (significantly) "secret": "I gave up much to be a companion to him in his suffering state. And oh! the groans and cries in secret that were raised in me, that I might be visited of the Lord, and come to knowledge of his way" (*EMP,* 39).

As Penington's narrative nears the Quaker years she resumes her emphasis on prayer. Prayer was her attempt to establish a private relationship with God, an endeavor that was to be her lifelong preoccupation though she had had only fleeting successes before she attended a Quaker meeting. "The soul in paraphrase, heart in pilgrimage," George Herbert had called prayer,[15] and for Mary it had been a long and lonely pilgrimage. A maidservant had read a very young Mary one of Preston's sermons that said that the hypocrite could not imitate the saint in true prayer. She became dissatisfied with set prayer, since the hypocrite could read it as well as the saint, but she was full of doubt about what true prayer was (*EMP,* 19). She tried writing her own prayers, but soon was more satisfied when, hearing of the sentencing of Prynne, Bastwick, and Burton to mutilation and banishment, she felt that her response was true prayer, the spontaneous outpouring of deep feeling: "I . . . kneeled down and poured out my soul in a very vehement manner. I was wonderfully melted and eased, and felt peace and acceptance with the Lord" (*EMP,* 21-2). But soon thereafter young Mary was deeply dissatisfied with her attempts to speak sincerely to God: "I mourned solely because I kneeled down morning after morning, and night after night, and had not a word to say. My distress was so great, that I feared I should perish in the night, because I had not prayed; and I thought that by day my food would not nourish me, because I could not pray" (*EMP,* 23). When, in her church-going years immediately following William's death, Mary zealously performed the approved religious duties including private prayer, she "thought no place too private to pray in, for I could not but be loud in the earnest pouring out of my soul," but she "could not find . . . answer of acceptation from the Lord" (*EMP,* 29–30). The spontaneity and vehemence of the "Prynne prayer" had become part of Mary's way of praying, but "acceptance with the Lord" had apparently not returned.

Shortly before the Quaker encounter began, Mary cried out to the Lord: "'it is acceptance with thee that I desire, and that alone can satisfy me'" (*EMP,* 39). In a culture that took issue with the Quakers almost wholly on doctrinal questions, when she first heard of them Mary Penington set aside doctrines and wished to apply her own touchstone: how they prayed. "Though I . . . despised this people, I had sometimes a desire to go to one of their meetings, if I could, unknown, and to hear them pray, for I was quite weary of doctrines; but I believed if I was with them when they prayed, I should be able to feel whether they were of the Lord or not" (*EMP,* 40). Praying, conversing with the Lord, was what mattered. Nowhere in the *Experiences* does Penington show the least interest in doctrine, not even Quaker formulations. Like the early Quakers, she seemed to know that no one was ever saved by getting doctrinal concerns right, and that all doctrinal understandings were merely verbal, "notional," unless they were incorporated in the heart.

The Quaker missionaries Thomas Curtis and William Simpson seem to be about to play a leading role in Mary Penington's convincement when she describes their appearance in her house: "I now knew that they came in the power and authority of the Lord." But being taught by human discourse is not Penington's way and the missionaries disappear from the narrative after Curtis repeats "this scripture, 'He that will know my doctrine, must do my commands'" (*EMP,* 42). Their visit is no more than a catalyst in Penington's convincement, which comes, as she tells it, after months of internal struggle to give effect to that scripture's commands by giving up her own life of privilege. Husband, friend, Quaker teacher – none has a place in her account of her effort to purge herself of the desire for the things that seem essential to her place in society. She sees what she must do, knowing that she can be assisted only by the Lord:

> I must come into a state of entire obedience before I could be in a capacity to perceive or discover what it was which they laid down for their principles. . . . Terrible was the Lord against the vain and evil inclinations in me, which made me, night and day, to cry out. . . .
>
> I never had peace or quiet from a sore exercise for many months, till I was . . . brought off from . . . deceit, bondage, and vanity, the spirit of the world, etc., and I given up to be a fool and a reproach, and to take up the cross to my honor and reputation in the world. (*EMP,* 43–4)

Having found herself able to repudiate "the language, fashions, customs, titles, honor, and esteem in the world" (*EMP,* 44), Penington now moves from solitary to communal worship and in a Quaker meeting has the assurance experience, "the purging of the heart, or answer of acceptation from the Lord" (*EMP,* 30) that she could never find in other congregations despite her zealous performance of all their prescribed duties. No longer ashamed to be seen at a Quaker meeting, she has one in her home. The Seeker vanishes along with the title and way of life of "Lady," and there is left only the "happy finder" of Cromwell's formulation:

> divested of reasonings, not consulting how to provide for the flesh, I received strength to attend the meetings of these despised people which I never intended to meddle with, but found truly of the Lord,

and my heart owned them. I longed to be one of them, and minded not the cost or pain. . . . Thus, by taking up the cross, I received strength against many things that I had thought impossible to deny; but many tears did I shed, and bitterness of soul did I experience, before I came thither . . . But oh! the joy that filled my soul in the first meeting ever held in our house at Chalfont. To this day I have a fresh remembrance of it. It was then the Lord enabled me to worship Him in that which was undoubtedly his own, and to give up my whole strength, yea, to swim in the life that overcame me that day. Oh! long had I desired to worship Him with acceptation, and lift up my hands without doubting, which I witnessed that day in that assembly. I acknowledged his great mercy and wonderful kindness; for I could say, "This is it which I have longed and waited for, and feared I never should have experienced." (*EMP*, 44–5)

This is, of course, the culmination of the narrative. The assurance experience is usually private, but as Penington presents the episode in her house the assurance experience and the worship carried on at the meeting seem to fuse, and it is not easy to separate the private from the public. She who has repudiated her due honors and fine clothing has reached a condition where she longs to be one of these despised people. It is "worship" that is the focus, and she feels assured that it is undoubtedly the kind of worship the Lord wishes, "his own," in which the worshiper surrenders individual strength to participate in the communal life of true worshipers. Ending her long pilgrimage, she swims in the life of being accepted by the Lord. Or, having given up her own strength (now seen as insufficient), does she swim in the divine life that has overcome her? Or, has she abandoned her singleness, the solitude that had failed her, to swim in the buoyant life of the meeting? These meanings overlap, perhaps because the experience encompasses all. What is clear is that the Mary Penington who resolved that she "would rather be without religion, until the Lord taught me one" (*EMP*, 39) now has learned a religion. It is Mary Penington as a worshiping being, a Quaker publicly worshiping "in that assembly," who is accepted by the Lord.

With this account of her convincement, Penington set aside her manuscript sometime before 1668 (*EMP*, 47–8). As it then stood the *Experiences* was a coherent and complete work that followed her spiritual development virtually to the exclusion of all her other affairs. The *Experiences* goes on, however, at some cost to the unity and effect of the memoir so well begun. Starting around October 1676, when she recorded an apocalyptic dream of uncertain significance, at various times Penington began to add material that she thought her loved ones might have an interest in. Since she had become settled in the Quaker faith, she felt free to write about matters that did not directly bear on her interior life. She describes the family's sufferings for the faith as relatives and tenants stripped Isaac of his property and rents, knowing that Quakers were helpless in the courts because they would not swear (*EMP*, 63). Having thus lost their house in Chalfont, Penington describes in some detail how she bought and supervised the rebuilding of a ruined house that became the family residence at Woodside (*EMP*, 55–62). She controls the whole financial and general contracting operation for this difficult, four-year project, showing a side of herself previously unhinted at. Besides a Mary Penington who takes quiet pride in her budgeting and management skills, a new style enters the memoir, one that abounds in named people, specific places, and the details of problems and costs.

What has become of the prose style that had characterized the narrative through the time of convincement, the spare style that so suppressed particularity about externals that even Mary's beloved husbands seem no more than extensions of her own thoughts and moods? The answer is, I believe, that Penington was ruled by her own sense of the decorum appropriate to her kind of spiritual autobiography. When she wrote about her fears, confusions, feelings, and motives in searching out a right relation to God, the external world mattered little and she found a language that focussed on the transactions of God in the heart. But it was not the only style she commanded. When in 1680 she wrote the encomiastic biographical memoir of Colonel William Springett that is her "A Letter . . . to . . . Springet Penn," she did not presume to portray William's inward spiritual states, but features the details of his evident virtues and great deeds. The letter bears no resemblance to what Jackson Cope would recognize as early Quaker prose style. One has only to read the episode of the perilous February journey in which Mary races by coach from London to Arundel in order to lay her cool kisses on the fevered lips of the dying William ("A Letter," in *EMP*, 86–95) to recognize that Penington is able to suit her style to her material. In "A Letter" she devotes over six pages to William dying in her presence, and both she and William are wonderfully realized; in the *Experiences* the moment is adequately noted by merely "my dear husband died" (*EMP*, 27).

Even while she was writing the copiously detailed "A Letter" in 1680, Penington brought back the spare style in the final pages of the *Experiences*, written in June and August of that year, and again in September 1681 and June 1682 (she died on 18 September 1682).[16] After the interlude telling of her family's sufferings for the faith and of housebuilding, Penington restores the setting that served so well to tell the story of her "experiences" from childhood through convincement. She is again a solitary figure in, as it were, a featureless landscape, without hill, tree, or fellow creature that might serve as reference points against which one might discern motion; the only motion to be narrated is interior motion within the solitary figure – her griefs, her physical agonies, her reaching a state that finds joy beyond sensual ease.

By 1680 Penington is through with writing of buildings and debts. She has settled her affairs and made her will. Isaac had died in 1679; since Mary reverts to her inward-looking style, her memoir says nothing about the manner of his death until, as we shall see, her memory of it impinges on her thoughts about her own death:

> And now I am mourning for the loss of my dear, worthy companion, and exercised with the great sickness and weakness of my children. . . . I have no great family to cumber me, am private, and have leisure to apply my heart to wisdom, in the numbering of my days to be but few. . . . I am waiting, sensible of the approach of death; having no desire after life, enjoying the satisfaction that I shall leave my children in an orderly way. . . . I feel that death is a king of terrors, and know that my strength to triumph over him, must be given by the Lord. . . . My sight to-day of things beyond the grave, will be insufficient in that hour, to keep me from the sting of death when he comes. It is the Lord alone will then be able to stand by me, and help me to resist the evil one, who is very busy when the tabernacle is dissolving. (*EMP,* 64–5)

The death of her husband and the sickness of her children enter the narrative not as phenomena having an interest in themselves that could deserve description and fill out a landscape, but as phenomena that are consequential only insofar as they occasion interior states in the solitary figure – her mourning, her worry, her satisfaction with feeling disencumbered. Death is a challenge to the figure's strength, reinforced by God's favor.

Penington's entries in the last two years of her life show her largely confined to her bed, intermittently racked by fever and excruciating "fits of the stone," but pleased that, through the power of God, "in all this time I have been a stranger to a murmuring, complaining mind" (*EMP,* 68–9). It is fitting that the *Experiences*, being an account of an effort from childhood through maturity to achieve a satisfying relationship with God, should, in its final entry, at the end of June 1682, show Penington to be in the state of "acceptation" that she had earlier declared to be the goal of her seeking: "'This is it which I have longed and waited for, and feared I should never have experienced'" (*EMP,* 45). Confined for many months to her bedchamber, Penington finds that being deprived of sleep, of the pleasures of eating, and of going "abroad in the air to view the beautiful creation" has heightened her spiritual pleasure:

> I have not asked anything of the Lord concerning life or health, but have rather felt pleasantness from being debarred from those things which are acceptable to the senses; because thereby I have been drawn nearer to the Lord, and have waited upon Him with much less distraction. . . . I have many times said, within myself: "Oh! this is sweet and easy. He makes my bed in my sickness, and withholds my eyes from sleeping, to converse with Him." (*EMP,* 69–70)

Thus has the seeker become the happy finder who, despite her acute pain, is in sweet and easy dialogue with the Lord. This could have been an inspirational point on which to close this memoir intended to benefit her children, confirming as it does the enduring value of faithfulness to Quaker ways. However, Penington adds two final paragraphs that reveal her sense of the mystery that carries to the last moments of human life, not to be illuminated on this side of the grave.

Although she delights in the comfort of her faith and retains her assurance that she has a heavenly destiny and will not die the second death, Mary Penington has been too long a Seeker to be complacent about her condition. She believes there is a final challenge that must be met since the dying moments of both Jesus and her husband Isaac indicate that even the spiritually strong cannot prepare themselves for all death's terrors:

> Even before I came to be settled in the truth, I entertained an awful sense of death, and was in subjection to the fear of it. But now that fear of death, and the state of death is removed; but there remaineth still a deep sense of the passage from time to eternity, how straight, hard, and difficult it is; and even many times to those on whom the second death hath no power, yet subjected to such feelings as were our dear Lord's and Savior's, when in agony he cried out: "My God! my God! why hast thou forsaken me?
>
> Another striking instance is that of my certainly blessed husband, whose mind was constantly with the Lord in his last illness; yet, when the last breath was breathing out, his groans were dreadful. I may call them roarings, as it seemed to be, through the disquiet of his soul at that moment. Indeed, this hard passage of his hath so deeply affected me, that I have often since said: "If it be thus with the green tree, how will it be with me, who am to him but as a dry tree." (*EMP,* 70–71)

Her memoir ends on this note of the indeterminate, confidence graced by humility before "the passage from time to eternity," a passage that is so incomprehensibly "straight, hard, and difficult" that it appears to have drawn a groan from even the exemplary Isaac's soul.

NOTES

1. *The Writings and Speeches of Oliver Cromwell*, ed. W.C. Abbott, 4 vols. (Cambridge: Harvard University Press, 1937–47), 1:416.
2. For a fine discussion of Cromwell's lack of interest in institutionalized religion, see especially pp.201–8 in J.C. Davis, "Cromwell's Religion," in *Oliver Cromwell and the English Revolution*, ed. John Morrill (London and New York: Longman, 1990), 181–208. Davis thinks Cromwell believed "that God would provide and that His custom was not to work through forms, institutions and rituals but inwardly through the hearts of men" (202).
3. *Experiences in the Life of Mary Penington (Written by Herself)*, ed. Norman Penney (1911; reprint, London: Friends Historical Society, 1992), 30–31. Citations from this edition will be incorporated in the text using the abbreviation *EMP*. The memoirs were first published in 1821.
4. In the period "notion" or "notional" was a popular, dismissive term for any idea or approach to a problem that, in the opinion of the user, experience showed to be without value. The term was frequently used by radical sectarians, for whom it was a term of abuse whose meaning shaded toward "imagination" or "imaginary." The antonyms were "experience" or "experimental." Thus those radicals who were satisfied with their access to the Spirit's teaching never tired of contrasting their knowing something "experimentally" and for certain with the merely "notional" knowledge of the learned clergy.
5. By the end of the decade that followed 1654, when the "Valiant Sixty" ministers left the North and spread throughout England and Wales, there were from 35,000 to 60,000 Quakers in the land, as numerous as Roman Catholics and more numerous than Baptists or Fifth Monarchists (Barry Reay, *The Quakers and the English Revolution* [London: Temple Smith, 1985], 11).
6. These and other facts about Mary Springett Penington given in this essay are either gleaned from her writings or taken from the Preface or Introduction to Penney's edition of the *Experiences* (x, 7–8, 10, 26–7).
7. Thomas Ellwood, *The History of the Life of Thomas Ellwood*, ed. C.G. Crump (London: Methuen, 1900), 9–12.
8. John Saltmarsh, *Sparkles of Glory, or Some Beams of the Morning Star* (1647; reprint London: William Pickering, 1847), 47. Saltmarsh provided a kind of theoretical structure for those who found they wanted to "progress" in spiritual knowledge. He elaborated on the Joachite tradition of the Three Ages (of Law, Gospel, and Spirit), identifying eight "dispensations" or stages in the historical development of Christianity, which stages are paralleled by the range of existing churches, which are in turn matched to the stages of religious development in the hearts of individual believers. Saltmarsh's eighth and final dispensation is one in which God himself directly ministers to the Sons of God; it is not only an eschatological event that ends time, but one that can be experienced now, at least in part and in glimpses, in the hearts of Saints: "And this Ministration is fulfilled then, when Christ shall have delivered up the kingdom unto God; and this is not only done upon the whole body of Christ at the last, but is fulfilled in its particular accomplishments, and mystery of Spirit here, there being found these transitions, passages, and resignations, and exchanges of glory in the Saint" (47).
9. *The Journal of George Fox*, ed. John L. Nickalls, rev. ed. (London: Religious Society of Friends, 1975), 21.
10. Quoted in Rufus M. Jones, *Studies in Mystical Religion* (London: Macmillan, 1936), 452. "Familists" was the favorite epithet for the orthodox to hurl against those they suspected of preferring their own "experiences" and illuminations by the Spirit to the teachings of learned

and beneficed clergy. The ubiquity of the epithet in the period supports my belief that the Seeker mood was widespread. Margaret Spufford observes that in Interregnum Cambridgeshire "the Baptist records give the impression that spiritual seeking and unrest was extremely widespread at the very lowest parochial level, amongst women and girls and laborers in the villages, and that the Quaker position was reached, or nearly reached, before the arrival of the Quakers" (*Contrasting Communities: English Villagers in the Sixteenth and Seventeenth Centuries* [London: Cambridge University Press, 1974], 283).

11. Laurence Clarkson, *The Lost Sheep Found* (1660; reprint, The Rota: University of Exeter, 1974), 4–34, 38.

12. Jackson I. Cope, "Seventeenth-Century Quaker Style," in *Seventeenth-Century Prose: Modern Essays in Criticism*, ed. Stanley E. Fish (New York: Oxford University Press, 1971), 203–4. Cope finds a similar effect in the prose of Stephen Crisp in 1694: "By insisting upon the spiritual experience, Crisp almost denies existence to the physical experience" (219).

13. Even long-time friends and fellow Friends like Ellwood are not referred to in the pre-Quaker portion of the *Experiences*. We learn from Ellwood that his family, living in London from about 1642 to the surrender of Oxford in 1646, were intimate friends of Lady Springett during that time (Ellwood, *Life*, 2), though it is not clear whether the friendship began before the death of her husband in February 1644 ("A Letter," in *EMP*, 95). In "A Letter" Penington gives an extended, detailed portrait of her mother-in-law, who continued to live with her after William's death until her own in 1647, and to practice healing and successful surgery on the eye and skull ("A Letter," in *EMP*, 73–7); she is clearly fond of this extraordinary, charitable woman and says "she always showed great kindness to me" ("A Letter," in *EMP*, 76), but Madam Springett earned no mention in the *Experiences*, where Penington stresses her solitary struggle.

14. Lucy Hutchinson, *Memoirs of the Life of Colonel Hutchinson*, ed. James Sutherland (London: Oxford University Press, 1973), 10.

15. "Prayer (I)" in *The Works of George Herbert*, ed. F. E. Hutchinson (Oxford: Clarendon, 1941), 51.

16. William I. Hull, *William Penn: a Topical Biography* (London: Oxford University Press, 1937), 36.

Handmaids of the Lord and Mothers in Israel:
Early Vindications of Quaker Women's Prophecy

ELAINE HOBBY

The importance of women's prophetical activity in the early years of the Society of Friends has long been noted: the first Quakers to preach in London and the English university towns, in Turkey, and in various parts of the Americas were female.[1] The missionary behavior of these women was endorsed by the fundamental Quaker insistence that every human being is inhabited by the Light, the first and final source of divine will. Moved by the Light, Friends of both sexes intervened in public discussion in person and in print, presenting their words not merely as divinely inspired, but as the actual voice of the Christ within them.[2] That Christ might be manifest in women as well as in men was to them axiomatic, though in the view of many of their contemporaries this contravened St Paul's injunction that "women keep silence in the churches" (1 Corinthians 34). Given this deviation from orthodox opinion, it is not surprising that from the 1650s onwards, brief defenses of female prophesying often appear in the midst of Quaker women's writings where the primary focus is on something else altogether. Writing from Newgate Prison in 1662, for instance, Hester Biddle speaks "as in Christ stead" (*The Trumpet Of the Lord Sounded forth* [London, 1662], 4) to deplore "the Sufferings of my People" (5), lamenting:

> Oh London! have not I who am the God of the whole World, placed a glorious burning Fire in thee. . . . I the Lord of Host [*sic*] hath caused my Sons, and Daughters, and Handmaids to leave both Father, and Mother, House and Land, Wife and Children. (4–5)

Comparable vindications in passing can be found in pamphlets as dissimilar as Sarah Blackborow's stormy warning, *The Just and Equal Balance Discovered* (London, 1660), and Anne Docwra's conciliatory, bookish *An Epistle of Love And Good Advice, To my old Friends & Fellow Sufferers in the Late Times, The Old Royalists And Their posterity* (London? 1680).[3]

Although justifications of women's preaching are commonplace in seventeenth-century Quaker tracts, from the beginning the mode of argumentation varies widely. This diversity itself indicates a fact long recognized but none the less not sufficiently heeded by historians: early Friends were gathered from a great variety of congregations and religious positions, some, like Elizabeth Hooton, already possessing noted reputations as preachers.[4] The theologies and related politics embraced by these early Friends may have changed through their involvement in the new movement, as they borrowed from and built on each others' ideas and experiences, but distinctions remained. This is manifest, for example, in the differences between the measured remonstrations of Ann Audland's *A True Declaration of the Sufferings of the Innocent* (London, 1655), and Dorothy White's ecstatic assertions in *A Diligent Search Amongst Rulers, Priests, Professors, and People* (London? 1659), that "all you high and loughty ones, you fruitless branches, you will the Lord cut down with the Sword of his power" (2). Later Quakerism, in contrast, tolerated a narrower range of prophetical voices.[5] A symptom of this contraction is the fact that William Sewell's *A History of the Rise, Increase, and Progress of the Christian People Called Quakers* (London, 1722), though rehearsing the by-then standard defense of women's speaking (volume 2: 416–17),[6] makes no mention of such fiery figures as Hester Biddle, Dewans Morey, or even Dorothy White, the second most prolific Quaker woman of the day, author of at least nineteen published pamphlets between 1659 and 1684.

This exclusion would seem to be connected to a fact that has often been remarked: when the Society of Friends metamorphosed from a fluid movement into an organized body, specific constraints with associated rights and duties were imposed on women members.[7] As participants in Women's Meetings, their identity was supposed to be defined not through preaching God's Word, but in providing material relief for poor Friends, placing female apprentices, prison visiting, examining the moral credentials of those seeking to marry, and so on: they were meant to be "mothers in Israel," to cite a much-used phrase. It was this post-Restoration retrenchment that produced the most-cited female defenses of women's speaking, Margaret Fell's *Women's Speaking Justified* (London, 1666, 1667), and Elizabeth Bathurst's *The Sayings of Women* (London, 1683). At first sight, these works might appear to contradict the assertion that the role of Quaker women was contracting, or their existence may itself seem to suggest a radical resistance to such change; and both, indeed, have often been interpreted in these ways.[8] However, once they are placed back in the context I have already mentioned, of widespread Quaker defense of the Spirit speaking in the female as well as in the male, their meaning appears to be somewhat other. Although both pamphlets cite detailed and wide-ranging scriptural precedents for female speech, they are careful and conservative in their claims and in the logic of their organization. They accept that only some women are permitted to speak, and then only in specific circumstances. Bathurst, for instance, opens her book by celebrating Sarah's defense of her son Isaac, and Rebecca's motherly care for Jacob in arranging his marriage (*The Sayings of Women,* 3–4). Fell is concerned to be explicit that the Inner Light cannot be used to excuse certain kinds of behavior:

> the Apostle permits not tatlers, busie-bodies [1 Timothy 5:13], and such as usurp authority over the Man [1 Timothy 2:10], would not have Christ Reign, to speak neither in the Male nor Female; Such the Law permits not to speak, such must learn of their Husbands [1 Corinthians 14:35]: But what Husbands have Widows to learn of, but Christ? And was not Christ the Husband of Philips four Daughters [Acts 21:9]? And may not they that learn of their Husbands speak then? (*Women's Speaking Justified,* 12)

This limited defense is consistent with the task of acting as "mothers in Israel" that post-Restoration Quaker women were supposed to undertake. Their role-model is the prophet Deborah, who sang as a "mother in Israel" (Judges 5:7) to celebrate her people's triumph in battle; not Jael, who helped achieve that victory by driving a tent-peg through Sisera's head (Judges 4:18–22).

To observe the limitations of Bathurst's and Fell's pamphlets is not to refuse their importance: they offered tools that their readers could use to justify women's speaking, and Scriptural traditions to argue from. What I am indicating is that these works are not radical in the way some have argued, and that there is no single or coherent tradition with which women's preaching was defended by Quakers. This variety is akin to the diverse stances from which the establishing of separate Women's Meetings was urged. Historians have attempted to find simple binary divisions between the group led by John Wilkinson and John Story, who opposed Women's Meetings, and followers of George Fox and Margaret Fell, who promoted their setting up. Any examination of the writings within which these positions were argued, though, indicates that different factions and individuals within the Society of Friends found themselves on the same side of this controversy for entirely incompatible reasons. For instance, Joan Vokins records her rapid return from the Americas in 1680 in order to defend the institution of "our Women's Meetings," before going on to spend her last ten years pursuing the old-style Quaker life of an itinerant preacher (*God's Mighty Power* [London, 1690], 29–31). Meanwhile, in 1685, William Loddington proposed that separate Women's Meetings should be encouraged as they could be an effective way of circumscribing and so reducing female power within the Society of Friends.[9] Where one saw a site of autonomy, the other perceived a means of containment.

No one familiar with the history of seventeenth-century Quakers will be surprised by these brief indications of change and variation in the movement, although some of the details noted here are not those usually focussed on. The particular interest of this paper, however, is not to add to the premature conclusions that have already been drawn concerning the precise historical role of women Quakers: the texts themselves are more diverse than existing accounts allow. Instead, I want to sketch what can be learnt through examining the widely diverse language used by those addressing the question of women's right to preach. Especially revealing are the ways in which different authors deploy biblical allusion; Quaker insistence that the Light Within supersedes the Word as the source of knowledge of God's will allowed the role accorded to the Bible to vary widely.[10]

Like some of their contemporaries, Friends justified their prophesying by reference to God's promise given in Joel 2:28, and repeated in Acts 2:17, that in the last days, "I will pour out my spirit upon all flesh; and your sons and your daughters shall prophesy." Also important was Paul's assertion in his letter to the "foolish Galatians" (Galatians 3:1), that "There is neither Jew nor Greek, there is neither bond nor free, there is neither male nor female: for ye are all one in Christ Jesus" (Galatians 3:28). These texts, and a network of other biblical mentions of female activity, some extremely brief, were all regularly cited as vindications of women's speaking. The need to rally such defenses was created in part by the fact that other bible verses enjoin female silence: most famously, St Paul in his epistles to the Corinthians and to Timothy:

> Let your women keep silence in the churches: for it is not permitted unto them speak; but they are commanded to be under obedience, as also saith the law. And if they will learn any thing, let them ask their husbands at home: for it is a shame for women to speak in the church. (1 Corinthians 14:34–5)

> Let the woman learn in silence with all subjection. But I suffer not a woman to teach, nor to usurp authority over the man, but to be in silence. (1 Timothy 2:11–12)

The effectiveness of the call to silence was much increased by other social factors. Being the Lord's handmaiden could have frightening consequences in a society which did not, in general, allow women to speak publicly or express opinions on religion or affairs of state, as is vividly documented in accounts of Quaker court trials. Before imprisoning Hester Biddle for prophesying in a Meeting in 1662, for instance, her jury asserted that "They never heard of a Woman to speak before" (*A Brief Relation of the Persecutions and Cruelties that have been acted upon the People called Quakers* [1662], 35); and when Sarah Tims was arrested in Banbury in 1655, the judge scolded her for questioning the legality of her jailing, informing her that "*sweeping the house, and washing the dishes was the first point of law to her*" (*The Saints Testimony* [London, 1655], 8).[11] Later that year when Dorothy Waugh was arrested for preaching in Carlisle, she was sentenced to the pain and humiliation of wearing a scold's bridle, and was ordered to be whipped (*The Lambs Defence* [London, 1656], 29–30). She was apparently undaunted: according to Sewell's *History*, in 1658 she traveled to Boston, Massachusetts, with a Friend, Sarah Gibbons. They were detained for speaking in church, "brought to the house of correction, and three days before their being whipped, and three days after, were kept from victuals, though they had offered to pay for them" (volume 1:251).[12]

In the face of such opposition, but guided by the Light, women did, however, produce dazzling defenses of their right to speak. Locked away in Exeter gaol in 1655, some eleven years before the appearance of Margaret Fell's *Women's Speaking Justified*, Priscilla Cotton and Mary Cole published a witty demolition of the argument that women should be silent in church. Their pamphlet is both a parody of the intellectualism of university men, and a display of their own confidence concerning the Bible's best interpretation. Adopting the rhetorical method of the early chapters of 1 Corinthians, which employs paradox and ironic exaggeration to undermine the Corinthians' beliefs,[13] and weaving together references to the gospels, Acts, and the Epistles, with arguments and promises taken from Amos, Numbers, Daniel and Chronicles, these women play a serious game with the meanings of words. Challenging the persecutors who have bidden them be silent and have imprisoned them, they compare university learning unfavourably with the wisdom of the women who accompanied Christ and his apostles, "silly women, as you would be ready to call them, if they were here now" (*To the Priests and People of England* [1655], 3, alluding to Luke 8:2). They demand:

> Come down thou therefore that hast built among the stars by thy arts and learning; for it's thy pride and thy wisdom, that hath perverted thee thou has gone in the way of *Cain*, in envy and malice, and ran greedily after the reward of *Balaam*, in covetousness, and if thou repent not, shalt perish in the gain-saying of KORE [Jude 11]. (5)

They proceed to apply this general argument to the specific scapegoating of Quakers, a device used by the powerful, Cotton and Cole claim, "that thy filthiness not be discovered, and thy shame appear" (6). The terms of this analysis are crucial to what follows. In speaking of their opponents' "filthiness" and "shame" they are following the common biblical and contemporary practice of comparing wrong-doers to adulterous women, whose shame is expounded upon by many biblical prophets in images with crude sexual resonances, most extensively in Ezekiel 23 and Revelation 17. This metaphorical equation of evil men and sexual women is then shifted by Cotton and Cole, however, as they reject any connection between gendered terms and the body, reproving their male oppressors, "thou sittest as a Queen and Lady over all" (6). From here, they build to an inexorable climax: the women forbidden to speak in the churches are not themselves, but university-educated ministers; in particular, the "women" who should be silent are the priests who have visited Cotton and Cole in prison to argue with them, men who "could not bear sound reproof and wholesome Doctrine . . . and so ran from us" (8).

To draw this conclusion, Cotton and Cole engage in an intellectual play which simultaneously displays their own familiarity with the Bible, and parodies the use made of it by the learned. Recalling Paul's advice to the Corinthians that "a woman may not prophesie with her head uncovered" (7, alluding to 1 Corinthians 11:5), they ignore for the moment the obvious evidence that the apostle here took for granted women's preaching, choosing instead to embark on a riotous game of paradox and irony. Just as their male opponents can be Queens and Ladies, so "head" means not part of the body, but Christ; neither men nor women can preach if not Christ-inspired. This established, they return to a brief catalogue of approved female teachers. Whichever way their opponents want to argue, women's right to speak cannot be denied:

> the Scripture saith, that a woman may not prophesie with her head uncovered, lest she dishonour her head: now thou wouldst know the meaning of that Head, let the Scripture answer, 1 *Cor.* 11.3. *The head of every man is Christ.* Man in his best estate is altogether vanity, weakness, a lye. If therefore any speak in the Church, whether man or woman, and nothing appear in it but the wisdom of man, and Christ, who is the true head, be not uncovered, do not fully appear, Christ the head is then dishonoured. Now the woman or weakness, that is man, which in his best estate or greatest wisdom is altogether vanity, that must be covered with the covering of the Spirit, a garment of righteousness, that its nakedness may not appear, and dishonour thereby come. Here mayst thou see from the Scriptures, that the woman or weakness whether male or female, is forbidden to speak in the Church; but its very plain, *Paul*, nor *Apollo*[*s*], nor the

true Church of Christ, were not of that proud envious Spirit that thou
art of, for they owned Christ Jesus in man or woman; for *Paul* bid
Timothy to help those women that laboured with him in the Gospel,
and *Apollo*[*s*] hearkened to a woman, and was instructed by her, and
Christ Jesus appeared to the women first, and sent them to preach the
Resurrection to the Apostles, and *Philip* had four Virgins that did
prophesie. (7)

Cotton and Cole's use of scripture here was certainly not original: at least
two years earlier Francis Higginson had attacked Quakers for claiming in
their meetings that the terms "male" and "female" need not refer to actual
men and women, but to the presence or absence of Christ in the person
speaking.[14] What is particular to the pamphlet, though, is the glee with
which they whirl through their argument, and the deftness with which they
slip in and out of their bibles. Such structures and tones are typical of the
work of a number of their direct female contemporaries – Dorothy White
and Hester Biddle as already mentioned, for instance, but also Margaret
Killin and Barbara Patison[15] – but is quite distinct from most other Quaker
writings focussed on the issue of women's speaking. For example,
Richard Farnworth is as careful and deliberative as Paul's Epistle to
Romans, the text from which he has taken most of his examples of women
speaking. But his parallel argument to the one quoted above becomes dull
in its repetitiveness and extraneous details:

> Now nothing is to speak in this Church which is spiritual, but that
> which is spiritual, even the Holy Ghost, which is invisible and
> incomprehensible; the Woman or wisdom of the Flesh is forbidden
> to speak in the Church, that is of the things of God, for that which is
> flesh is flesh, and the natural man he knows not the things of God,
> they are foolishness to him, neither can he know them because they
> are spiritually discerned, 1 *Cor.* 4. and so the carnal minded man he
> sayeth, that a Woman (or the female kinde) ought not to speak in the
> Church: now the first birth either in man or woman hath nothing to
> do to speak in the Church, (the carnal part) for it knows not the
> things of God, and every man by nature is a childe of wrath, and he
> is forbidden to speak with his carnal wisdom, which he gathered out
> of Books and Studyes for that nature is adulterated from God, and
> nothing must speak in the Church in God but the Holy Ghost, and
> that may speak in the Temple, either in male or female; nothing must
> speak in the Church, but the Spirit of Truth, whom the world and
> carnal minded ones know not. (*A Woman forbidden to speak In the
> Church* [London, 1654], 2)

George Fox's *The Woman Learning in Silence* (1656), proceeds differently again. He structures his argument through a series of propositions and counter-propositions, quoting conventional thinking and then swiping it away for its inconsistency with some other part of Scripture. As Cotton and Cole repeat words such as "woman" or "head," meanings slide and redefine. Fox works in the manner of traditional rhetoric, by repetition and inversion. Where Cotton and Cole demolish all social hierarchies, insisting "there is no respect of persons with God" (8), Fox continues to embrace differences in gender roles: women are saved through child-bearing, not through being inhabited by the Light. Indeed, his pamphlet opens:

> Let your women learn in silence, with all subjection; here is a silent learning, a learning in silence: I suffer not a woman to Teach, nor to usurp Authority over the man, but to be silent, there she is to learn, in the silence, and not to usurp Authority over the man, but ask her Husband at home. That which usurps Authority, the Law takes hold on, but if you be led of the spirit, then you are not under the Law: So I permit not a Woman to speak in the Church, as saith the Law: So let the Women learn in silence, with all subjection: But I suffer not a woman to usurp Authority over the man, but be in all silence; for *Adam* was formed, then *Eve* and *Adam* was not deceived, but the woman was in the Transgression, Read 1 *Tim.* 2. Nevertheless she shall be saved in child-bearing, if she continue in faith and charity, and holiness, and sobriety. (1)[16]

Although this brief essay has looked only at writings concerned with women's preaching, I want to end by making a couple of broader points. First, I am suggesting that a more detailed engagement with particular texts can provide a sense of the range of politics embraced by early Quakers. So many of these writings are only available in a few specialist libraries that they remain largely unread, and modern accounts of Friends' history, despite their strengths, generalize on the basis of reading too few authors. At the same time, unfortunately, some attempts to awaken critical interest in these works seem misinformed or misdirecting. There has been a tendency amongst those questioning the literary canon's boundaries to take one of two lines when making reference to Quaker pamphlets. Some follow the lead set by Elaine Showalter in her pioneering book *A Literature of Their Own*, and look for a single, interlinked tradition of suppressed texts.[17] Mary Anne Schofield, for instance, wants to find in the writings of Elizabeth Bathurst, Joan Vokins, Elizabeth Stirredge, and others, signs that they were writing the precursors of eighteenth-century women's novels. To do this requires erasing the political movement within which Quaker women were writing, seeing this source of the texts as producing merely a "surface" narrative (68). Schofield then ignores the pamphlets' rich Song of Solomon resonances in order to see their references to gardens as exempla of the gardens of romance.[18] Another favored approach is to apply post-Lacanian theory to early Quaker prophecies. This project results in the endless repetition that radical texts display a plethora of voices erupting through the symbolic order to produce "feminine" utterance.[19] Both approaches deny the texts their material specificity: these pamphlets are not consistent with each other in content or form, but neither do they exhibit surging difference.

For the validity of these assertions to be tested, we need good modern editions of these seventeenth-century breakings of silence; now.

NOTES

1. William C. Braithwaite, *The Beginning of Quakerism* (London: Macmillan, 1912), 158–9; Hugh Barbour, "Quaker Prophetesses and Mothers in Israel," in *Seeking the Light*, ed. by J.W. Frost and J.M. Moore (Wallingford and Haverford, Pennsylvania: Pendle Hill Publications and the Friends' Historical Association, 1986); Phyllis Mack, *Visionary Women: Ecstatic Prophecy in Seventeenth-Century England* (Berkeley and Oxford: University of California Press, 1992).

2. Useful discussion of the early Quaker concept of the Light Within appears in Maurice A. Creasey, "'Inward' and 'Outward': A Study of Early Quaker Language," *Journal of the Friends' Historical Society*, Supplement 30 (1962); Mack, *Visionary Women*, 7; Barry Reay, *The Quakers and the English Revolution* (London: Temple Smith, 1985). Richard Bauman, *Let Your Words Be Few: Symbolic Speaking and Silence among Seventeenth Century Quakers* (London: Cambridge University Press, 1983), explores Friends' simultaneous commitment to the importance of not speaking, since only in silence could the small still voice of Christ be heard and hence relayed.

3. See also, for instance, Dorcas Dole, *Once More* (London?, 1683); Katherine Evans, *A Brief Discovery* (London, 1663); Margaret Fell, *An Evident Demonstration* (London, 1660); Rebecca Travers, *Of That Eternal* (London? 1659); Joan Vokins, *A Loving Advertisement* (London? 1671); Dorothy White, *A Visitation* (London, 1660); Jane Whitehead *et al.*, *For The King* (London? 1670); Isabel Yeamans, *An Invitation of Love* (London? 1679).

4. The range of Quaker origins is catalogued in Braithwaite, *Beginning*, 60, and in Reay, *Quakers*, chapter 1. Mack, *Visionary Women*, argues that there are broad differences between northern and southern Quaker women, but I am convinced neither by her categories nor by her evidence. Elizabeth Hooton's importance is argued for in Emily Manners, *Elizabeth Hooton, first Quaker woman preacher (1600–1672)* (London: Headley Brothers, 1914).

5. Fox could be one crucial instrument of this narrowing of the bounds of Quakerism, since according to Hugh Barbour, *Margaret Fell Speaking* (Pendle Hill: Pendle Hill Pamphlet no. 206, 1976), 21, he himself sorted and labeled Quaker manuscripts in 1675–76. Certainly Thomas Ellwood's edition of Fox's posthumously published *Journal* (London, 1694) volume 2: 3, accelerated any such contraction of Quaker profile through a number of omissions, for instance of any mention of the voluminous writings of Katherine Evans and Sarah Cheevers, although Fox's part in winning their release from the inquisition in Malta is given in detail.

6. References to Sewell's *History* given here are to the edition published in two volumes in Philadelphia, c. 1856.

7. On the development of the Quakers from a fluid movement to an organized body, see T.P.

O'Malley, "'Defying the Powers and Tempering the Spirit'. A Review of Quaker Control over their Publications 1672–1689," *The Journal of Ecclasiastical History*, Vol.33 No.1 (1982): 72–88; Reay, *The Quakers*. For the impact of such changes on women, see William C. Braithwaite, *The Second Period of Quakerism* (London: Cambridge University Press, second edition, 1961); Mabel Brailsford, *Quaker Women 1650–1760* (London: Duckworth and Company, 1915); Elaine Hobby, *Virtue of Necessity: English Women's Writing 1649–1688* (London: Virago, 1988); Mack, *Visionary Women*; Christine Trevett, *Women and Quakerism in the Seventeenth Century* (York: The Ebor Press, 1991); Bonnelyn Young Kunze, *Margaret Fell and the Rise of Quakerism* (London: Macmillan, 1994).

8. Fell's *Women's Speaking Justified* is commonly but wrongly lauded as the first female defense of women's preaching. See, for instance, Susan Mosher Stuard, "Women's Witnessing: A New Departure," in *Witnesses for Change: Quaker Women Over Three Centuries* (New Brunswick and London: Rutgers University Press, 1989), 3–25; David Latt, *Women's Speaking Justified (Margaret Fell, 1667), Epistle from the Women's Yearly Meeting at York, (1688), A Warning to All Friends (Mary Waite, 1688)*, (The Augustan Reprint Society Publication no. 194, 1979); Mary Anne Schofield, "'Women's Speaking Justified': The Feminine Quaker Voice, 1662–1797," *Tulsa Studies in Women's Literature* 6 (1987): 61–77; Margaret Hope Bacon, *Mothers of Feminism: The Story of the Quaker Women in America* (San Francisco and London: Harper and Row, 1986). This insistence on Fell's precedence is particularly striking in the light of the fact that Braithwaite, *Beginning*, is explicit that Fell's work was by no means the first of its kind.

9. Loddington is quoted in Mack, *Visionary Women*, 228; see also her discussion of the anti-women sentiments of Hugh Wood, Richard Smith, and William Matter (291). Mack's interpretation of the debate over Women's Meetings differs fundamentally from mine: implicitly borrowing post-Lacanian concepts, she sees such meetings as nurturing an archetypal and liberating feminine, and especially maternal, energy. George Fox insists in his *Journal*, volume 2: 342–3, that the establishing of Women's Meetings was his own idea. The account he gives, however, indicates that the initiative first came from Sarah Blackborow, and that her concern was to take action against pressing poverty in London. Certainly such an emphasis would be consistent with the priorities revealed in her published writings.

10. Useful studies of Quaker style include Jackson I. Cope, "Seventeenth-Century Quaker Style," *PMLA* 71 (1956): 725–54; Creasey, "'Inward' and 'Outward'"; Luella Wright, *The Literary Lives of the Early Friends, 1650–1725* (New York, Columbia University Press, 1932). See also Paul Christianson, *Reformers and Babylon: English Apocalyptic Visions from the Reformation to the Eve of Civil War* (Toronto: University of Toronto Press, 1978). It is frequently asserted that, owing to their emphasis on the Inner Light, Quakers made little use of the Bible. In *The Quakers*, 34, Reay claims Christopher Hill's *The World Turned Upside Down* as an authority for this position, but Hill's own reading of Quaker texts there, as elsewhere, is far more careful and multi-layered than this.

11. Debates over women's speaking also raged in Baptist congregations. See Susanna Parr, *Susanna's Apology* (London? 1659) (or the extract printed in *Her Own Life: Auto-biographical Writings by Seventeenth-Century Englishwomen*, edited by Elspeth Graham *et al*. [London, Routledge, 1989]). See also the limits placed on women's right to speak in John Rogers, *Ohel or Beth-shemesh* (London, 1653), 463 (misnumbered 563)–77.

12. See also Barbara Blaugdone, *An Account of the Travels, Sufferings & Persecutions* (London, 1691), which details years of punishments for preaching. It is important to note when reading these materials that male Quakers might have suffered even more severely: according to Braithwaite, *Second Period*, more men than women were punished under the Quaker Act in 1662, and in the widespread persecution of Friends in 1686, only about 200 of the 1383 Quakers in prison were women (109).

13. Creasey's "'Inward' and 'Outward'" discusses the appeal of 1 Corinthians 4 to early Quaker polemicists.

14. Francis Higginson, *A Brief Relation of the Irreligion of the Northern Quakers* (London, 1653), cited in Mack, *Visionary Women*: "one Williamson's wife . . . said in the hearing of divers [people] . . . that she was the eternal Son of God; And when the men that heard her, told her that she was a woman, and therefore could not be the Son of God: She said, no, you

are women, but I am a man" (157).

15. See especially Dorothy White, *A Call from God Out of Egypt* (London, 1662), where she picks up Cotton and Cole's argument; Margaret Killin and Barbara Patison, *A Warning from the Lord to the Teachers & People of Plimouth* (London? 1655); and Hester Biddle, *Wo to thee City of Oxford* (London, 1655) an edited version of which is given in full in Elaine Hobby, "'Oh Oxford thou art full of filth': the prophetical writings of Hester Biddle, 1629(?)–1696," in *Feminist Criticism: Theory and Practice*, edited Susan Sellers (London: Harvester Wheatsheaf, 1991), 157–70.

16. William Adamson, *An Answer* (London, 1656), 8–9, is markedly similar in his structure and argument. For a stimulating analysis of Fox's rhetorical method, see Jackson I. Cope, "Seventeenth-Century Quaker Style," *PMLA* 71 (1956): 725–54.

17. Elaine Showalter, *A Literature of Their Own: British Women Novelists from Brontë to Lessing* (London: Virago, 1977).

18. Mary Anne Schofield, "'Women's Speaking Justified': The Feminine Quaker Voice, 1662–1797," *Tulsa Studies in Women's Literature* 6 (1987): 61–77.

19. See Christine Berg and Philippa Berry, "'Spiritual Whoredom': An Essay on Female Prophets in the Seventeenth Century," in *1642: Literature and Power in the Seventeenth Century*, ed. by Francis Barker *et al.* (Essex: University of Essex, 1981). Similar readings are echoed in Schofield, "Women's Speaking"; Mack, *Visionary Women*; Margaret Ezell, *Writing Women's Literary History*, Baltimore and London: The Johns Hopkins University Press, 1993.

"No Man's Copy":
The Critical Problem of Fox's Journal

THOMAS N. CORNS

And though the side of his understanding which lay next to the world, and especially the expression of it, might sound uncouth and unfashionable to nice ears, his matter was nevertheless very profound; and would not only bear to be often considered but the more it was so the more weighty and instructing it appeared. And abruptly and brokenly as sometimes his sentences would fall from him about divine things, it was well known they were often as texts to many fairer declarations. And indeed it showed, beyond all contradiction, that God sent him, that no arts or parts had any share in his matter or manner of his ministry; and that so many great, excellent, and necessary truths as he came forth to preach to mankind had therefore nothing of man's wit or wisdom to recommend them; so that as to man he was an original, being no man's copy.[1]

Penn's shrewd comments of 1694 alert the modern critic to quite how difficult it proves to develop a critical perspective on Fox's *Journal*. In part the problem rests in the contrast between Fox's awesome powers as charismatic religious leader and his perfunctory involvement in his later years in the cool medium of printed prose. Certainly he was a frequent and sometimes powerful controversialist, but those activities which most strongly distinguished him for his contemporaries and followers, the extraordinary powers he showed in the "convincement" of converts to Quakerism, both in private meetings and through sermons, are scarcely captured in print. Quaker sermons from the early period have all but disappeared; only one survives from the first two decades of the movement, and indeed Quaker commitment to impromptu composition and hostility to the printed sermon acted strongly against the survival of such speech-acts.[2] Fox's own account of the convincements he wrought, while sometimes rich in circumstantial detail, rarely relates what he said. The following is about as full an account of the process as we find:

Soe I declared to ye people: y^t I came not to holde uppe there Idolls temple nor tyths nor preists but to declare against y^m: & opned to ye

> people all there traditions: & y^t peice of Grounde was noe more holy then another peice of Grounde: & y^t they should know y^t there bodyes were to bee ye temples of God & Christ & soe to bringe y^m of all ye worlds hirelinge teachiers to Christ there free teacher: & directinge y^m to ye Spiritt & grace & ye light of Jesus y^t they might knowe both God & Christ & ye Scriptures & soe passed away quiett & many was convinced there.[3]

Fox contextualizes the conversion process in an anti-clerical assault, characteristic of many radical puritans, on tithes and a professional clergy; how this works so efficiently on the consciousness of his hearers remains a mystery. And indeed, more characteristically, Fox foregrounds the mysteriousness of his impact on those he converts, reducing his own role to that of the agency bringing the spirit within himself into proximity with the converts:

> And wee sent to ye ranters to come foorth & try there God & there came aboundans whoe was rude as aforesaid: & sunge & whistled & danced but ye Lords power soe confounded y^m y^t many of y^m came to be convinct.
>
> And after this I came to Twy Crosse & there came some ranters againe & they sunge & danced before mee but I was moved in ye dreade of ye Lord to speake to y^m & reprove y^m & ye Lords power came over y^m soe as some of y^m was reacht & convinced & received ye spiritt of God & are come to bee a pretty people.... (I: 152)

Fox makes no attempt to relate the working of the spirit. Probably he would have regarded such an attempt as beyond the range of what human language can achieve. The devotional practices and exercises of early Quakers placed silent waiting on the spirit at the center of religious experience. As Bauman summarizes Quaker practice, "Silence is both antecedent to speaking in worship and the end of speaking in worship; silence precedes speaking, is the ground of speaking, and is the consequence of speaking."[4] Or as the Quaker Charles Marshall put it in 1677, once you have spoken, "retire inward, and sink down into the pure stillness, and keep in the Valley."[5]

This privileging of silence over speech is at the level of theory a privileging of the speech of the inner spirit, articulated in silence, over human speech; as the believer falls silent, he or she may hear and may transmit that inner voice. It is wholly consonant with such views that Fox should refrain from trapping in human speech in written form that voice he found or, as he would suggest, found him in the exigencies of dozens of conversion episodes.

But besides the Quaker respect for silence, another notion, one which unites Fox with other religious radicals including those Ranters among whom he proselytized with such good effect, shapes this relegation of human speech. That is, the recognition of the inadequacy of human discourse for representing the voice of the spirit and the truth it vouchsafes. There are analogies in the writings of Richard Coppin, who, though he denied being a Ranter, "was influential among Ranters; and it is difficult to think of any label which would describe him better."[6] Coppin argued that truth was incapable of being embodied in any outward form, arguing for the limitations of human discourse in communicating the central truths of divine transcendence:

> to know the Original of Truth, is to know God himself, for the Original is the truth of all things; and God is the Original and this Truth: for he is before all things and is all things, and is the end of all things; as it is said, *The end of all things is at hand*; and this end is God, who is not seen, not comprehended by anything, but by himself.[7]

I suppose Coppin means that only the spirit within, which is coessential with the godhead, may "comprehend" the godhead. University-trained intellectuals of the paradoxical proclivities of Coppin or the Ranter leader Abiezer Coppe, who wrote a preface to his *Divine Teachings*, may seek to articulate in language the inadequacies of language for spiritual truth. Fox, whose robust mind is never drawn to such paradox, leaves the issue as a signifying silence at the center of his *Journal*. Thus while he may give names and dates and places of those occasions when the spirit within him reached out to convince others, that process remain unarticulated; his account leaves us such circumstantial narration, like an empty cocoon evidencing the departure of the creature it once held. Hill too has remarked on the disparity between Fox's account of events and his evident impact on large meetings.[8]

Indeed, Fox's account sometimes works to define the enigmas of the spirit's operation. Consider perhaps the *Journal*'s most vivid episode, his visitation of Lichfield. On seeing at some remove the distinctive three spires of the cathedral[9] (more steeples than most steeplehouses possess), he is moved by "the worde of ye Lord" to go there. He bids his companions leave him:

> assoone as they was gonne for I saide nothing to y^m {whethre I would goe} butt I went over hedge & ditch till I came within a mile of Lichfeilde & when I came Into a great feilde wher there was

shepheards keepinge there sheepe I was commanded of ye Lorde to
putt of my shooes off a sudden & I stoode still & ye word of ye
Lorde was like a fire in mee & beinge winter I untyed my shooes &
putt y^m off: & when I had donne I was commanded to give y^m to ye
shepheards [& was to charge y^m to lett noe one have y^m except they
paide for y^m].

And ye poore shepheards trembled & were astonished & soe I
went about a mile till I came Into ye townde & asoone as I came
within ye townde ye worde of ye Lorde came unto mee againe to cry:
Woe unto ye bloody citty of Lichfeilde: soe I went uppe & doune ye
streets cruinge Woe unto ye bloody citty of Lichfeilde & beinge
markett day I went Into ye markett place & went uppe & doune in
severall places of it & made stands crying Woe unto ye bloody citty
of Lichfeilde & noe one touched mee nor layde hands off mee.

[And soe att last some freindes & freindely people came to mee
& said alacke George where is thy shooes & I tolde y^m Itt was noe
matter] soe when I declared what was upon mee & cleared my selfe
I came out of ye tounde in peace about a mile to ye shepheards: &
there I went to y^m & tooke my shooes & gave y^m some money & ye
fire off ye Lorde was soe In my feete & all over mee y^t I did not
matter to putt my shooes one any more & was att a stande whether I
shoulde or noe till I felt freedome from ye Lorde soe to doe. (I: 15)

Hill remarks of the passage of analysis Fox appends to this narrative that
"Fox felt it necessary, long after the event, to rationalize his behaviour in
Lichfield, singularly unconvincingly."[10] Certainly, Fox represents himself
as pondering why he should have behaved thus *here*, and offers the view
that he had been moved to go in his stockings through the market place
because historically that was the site in the time of Diocletian of the
martyrdom of numerous Christian Britons. Yet Hill's comments seem
perhaps a little jaundiced. It is more coherent to conclude that Fox is
trying to make sense of the incident for himself rather than to explain
away an episode embarrassing to the movement on the eve of the age of
reason. For Fox retains within the primary account, despite its gloss,
powerful elements of enigma and bewilderment. Early Quakers (though
not Fox) sometimes "went naked for a sign" (a practice Hill rightly
connects with the Lichfield episode).[11] This practice of appearing
unclothed and indeed sometimes stark naked in public places seems to
have been supported by a variety of explanations offered by practitioners
and was subject to varied and bewildered hostile comment by non-Quaker
contemporaries.[12] What is oddest about Fox's account of the Lichfield
episode (and what his rationalization seeks to address) is the detail of his

shoes. Within the narrative it is the focus of practical attention (paradoxically, in the relating of so impractical a decision): Fox finds some shepherds to look after them for him, and he arranges that they will retain them till he comes back and gives them money in fee for their service. It leads him to reflect, in a complete absence of a sense of irony, that his feet didn't get cold while he was walking around barefoot because "ye fire of ye Lorde was soe In my feete." He courts absurdity and he vouchsafes an account of youthful zeal beyond rational constraint. This does not sound like a man cleaning up the record before disclosing it to a public for whom Quakerism must be made respectable. Rather the narrative retains a commitment to relating the operation of the spirit within in all its opacity to human understanding. Note how the other figures in this landscape, the shepherds who tremble at him and his friends who express concern about the whereabouts of his shoes, throw into sharp definition the eccentricity of his own actions.

Indeed, the curious things the spirit makes him do whirl through his *Journal* in major incidents and trifles. On his journeys the spirit constrains him to test a woman who had denied him milk by asking for cream, which she also claims not to have but which a child promptly upsets: "& soe I walkt out of her house after ye Lord God had manifested her deceite & perversenesse," leaving the woman "amased" (I: 20). Another time, he casts his eye "upon an uncleane woman," and is prompted "in ye Lords power" to speak sharply to her, after which she is recognized in her own community as a witch (I: 113). The spirit prompts him to reprove "a Lady" who would cut his hair (I: 285). But the spirit acts, too, on the global scale, enabling the incarcerated Fox to witness visions of the halt of the Turkish incursion into Europe and the beginning of the Second Anglo-Dutch War (II: 89-90). Even in retrospect and some years from the event, Fox never seeks to moderate the strangeness of the spirit's prompting within him.

Penn's portrait of Fox depicts him as someone distinguished by the power of that spirit within. It depicts him also as someone disinclined to finish the task of writing, leaving that to others: "abruptly and brokenly ... his sentences would fall from him." Indeed so, and the manuscript legacy which became his *Journal* posed a considerable task for those charged with the responsibility of preparing it for its eventual publication in 1694. The manuscript which survives is the three-volume Spence manuscript in the possession of the Friends' Library, London.[13] How the manuscript relates to the first edition is uncertain. Most likely Thomas Ellwood, who had primary responsibility for that edition, transcribed or caused to be transcribed the Spence manuscript, in the process regularizing punctuation and spelling along the lines of contemporary printing-house practice and in various ways softening the idiom, toning down the millenarian rhetoric, and adjusting the text to the politics and taste of the 1690s, as later editors have remarked.[14] Interestingly, some of the early part of the Spence MS is endorsed on alternate sheets with the marginal note "done" in what appears to be a seventeenth-century hand, in a way which suggests those sheets were originally folio booklets; "done" perhaps signifies they have been transcribed. Ellwood would seem to have had some access to material not in the Spence MS. Also, the early section of the Spence MS, corresponding to the first thirty pages of the 1694 edition, is not extant.

Whatever the editorial mediation of Quakers after Fox's death, there is ample evidence that the *Journal* had a complicated but uncertain history in manuscript.The date and circumstances of its composition remain speculative. Thomas Lower, Fox's son-in-law, was the principal amanuensis, and since it would be reasonable to assume the composition of the *Journal* was the work of several months it has often been suggested that it must have been the work of one of the periods when both men lived in proximity, either during their incarceration together in Worcester jail or during a sojourn at Swarthmore Hall in 1675–77. Penney argues convincingly for the later window, and Ingle concurs.[15] Whichever was the period of primary composition, there is evidence of considerable revision to the manuscript. Most obviously, there are numerous interlineal and marginal additions, usually of supplementary material which clarifies or augments the narrative or disambiguates the text. These are often in a hand other than Lower's. Again, some pages which are in Lower's hand have the sort of cramping of their concluding lines which would indicate a recopying of some sheets to assimilate material that has been added.[16] Again, the task facing Ellwood was to produce a coherent journal by incorporating various letters to and from Fox and other documents into the principal narration of events. Many of these documents appear in the Spence manuscript in an approximately appropriate point in the narrative sequence. However, it is obvious that some were added to the narration somewhat earlier than others. The clearest evidence comes from a wormhole which runs in the middle of the page through volume one from the first manuscript page to folio 92. It passes through most inserted epistolary material, but not through the letter on folios 575-58. Thus the papers which make up that part of the Spence manuscript must once have contained some letters but not others, evidence of editorial or possibly authorial tinkering with the manuscript at a stage between its composition and its transcription.

This complex but shadowy history has distinct implications for the ideological interpretation of the *Journal*. Radical activists of the mid-century, in the puritans' winter of the 1660s and early 1670s, told and re-told the experiences of earlier days in a ways which comment eloquently on the poignant but unstable circumstances in which they found themselves. Thus, in the case of the generically analogous Bunyan text, *Grace Abounding to the Chief of Sinners*, while the earliest edition represents an intrepid but introverted commitment to internalized resistance, subsequent editions, especially after the initiative towards dissenters of 1672, seek to represent anabaptists in more politic fashion as respectable protestants distinct from groups like Quakers and Ranters and as people prepared to live peaceably with the Restoration ascendancy.[17] It may well be possible to reconcile the ideological despondency of *Paradise Lost* with the assured passivity of *Paradise Regained* and the militant confidence in returning power celebrated in *Samson Agonistes* through similar reference to the despair of the mid-1660s and the recognition in the early 1670s that the restored order was not so secure nor so implacably certain that dissent should and could be extirpated.[18]

Some have attempted to read the *Journal* as Fox's attempt to clean up the radical past of Quakerism (much as Bunyan in later editions of *Grace Abounding* cleaned up anabaptism), and thus to render it tolerable to those in power. Such an argument underlies much of Hill's influential account of Fox in *The World Turned Upside Down*. Hill persistently asserts "This is not to suggest anything like deliberate distortion: simply that the story looks different when you know, or think you know, how it ended." But he goes on, "Thus in Fox's *Journal* James Nayler plays a part only slightly greater than that of Trotsky in official Soviet histories of the Russian Revolution";[19] inevitably one must wonder whether the analogy figures Fox as Lenin or Stalin, and inevitably one rather gravitates towards the latter. Fox's latest biographer interprets the *Journal* as a complex polemic designed to assert Fox's place within the movement in the 1670s and to allow him to jerk the choke-chain on more radical elements within it:

> Over the course of his half-century Fox had learned that control of the past allowed a person to grasp the present and shape the future. ... The *Journal*'s backdrop was the conflict raging among Friends. Plumbing his memory, Fox found weapons to hurl at opponents. ... He calculatedly wrote minor dissidents out of his movement's history or reduced their roles. He grouped some lesser figures with major challengers like Nayler and Perrot and, lest his judgment be questioned, reduced the roles of friends ... [who] had since become his enemies. ... his memoir was as polemical as anything he ever wrote.
>
> It also served to distort the actual record, for Fox naturally placed himself at the center of the movement, even in the 1660s and 1670s when his travels to the colonies, lengthy imprisonments, and

debilitating illnesses forced him to step aside and permit others to bear more responsibility for the Quaker sect.[20]

Again, the allusion to *1984* perhaps unfortunately rehearses the Fox–Stalin analogy. Committed though I am to skeptical readings exposing covert tendencies in texts, I find it hard to read the *Journal* thus. A polemical impulse may well have been among those factors motivating Fox, but this, if it is indeed polemic, is muffed polemic, a stratagem not carried through to completion. The work as Fox left it was plainly some way from press-readiness, nor could he leave it alone, as the state of the manuscript plainly shows. Thus we see him picking it over, revising it, having bits rewritten and documents newly inserted. Civil War polemic and its Restoration legacy constitute material of great immediacy, no sooner written than published, no sooner published than read, no sooner read than discarded. This great volume, eventually published post-humously as a rather grand folio, is written to a different rhythm. However devaluative of early comrades and their contribution, it can scarcely in Fox's lifetime have made a jot of difference to his place in Restoration Quakerism, nor was the text stabilized in Fox's lifetime. (Though it may well be argued that it is a tract that shows some concern with the responses of posterity.)

Moreover, it inadvertently displays (as Robert Burton might have put it, it anatomizes) the contradictions at the heart of Fox's ideology. If there is a larger political argument, it is that Quakers are not to be persecuted by Charles II's apparatuses of state because they were persecuted by the English Republic's corresponding apparatuses, a species of the argument that your enemy's enemy is your friend (one of the sillier ideas of late-twentieth-century *Realpolitik* and one which Charles II was far too astute to give assent to; he well knew that some of Cromwell's enemies were his enemies also).

Nevertheless, with varying degrees of conviction, Fox works through the demonology of Restoration royalism. Thus he selects in his anecdotes from the 1650s figures of Restoration notoriety. Colonel Francis Hacker, who had commanded the guards at the execution of Charles I and who was executed at the Restoration, is depicted both manifesting his hostility of Quakerism and living (briefly) to regret it:

And soe I desired they would lett mee speake with Coll Hacker & hee had me to his bed syde: & hee was at mee againe to goe home & keepe noe more meetinges & I tolde him I coulde not submitt to y[t] but must have my liberty to serve God & goe to meetinges.
Then hee saide I must goe before O: {L[d]} P{[r]}: soe I kneeled one

his bed syde & desired ye Lord to forgive him for hee was Pilate though hee woulde wash his hands. And when ye day of his misery & tryall should come upon him I then bid him remember what I saide to him. . . .

Now when this Coll: Hacker was in ye tower of London: a day or two before hee was hanged Itt was tolde him what hee had donne against ye innocent & hee remembred it & confesst to it to Margarett ffell & saide hee knew well {whome she meant}. (I: 160, 162)

Yet as polemic designed to moderate royalist oppression, it is less than felicitous: *imitatio Christi* martyrdom had since 1649 been perceived as the role of Charles I.[21] Again, royalists may well have thought Hacker's unsympathetic treatment of Fox (a pale and penalty-free version of the banning of conventicles so central to Restoration anti-dissenter legislation) was somewhat trivial compared with supervising Charles I's execution, a more appropriate event for a meditation before Tyburn.

Perhaps the treatment of Vane works a little better. A particular *bête noire* of Charles II,[22] Vane in Fox's narrative emerges as insufferably arrogant:

And then hee remembred my words & confessed his mistake but hee grew Into a great frett & a passion....

And soe I went away & hee saide to some frends afterwards y' if Anthony Peason & some others had not beene with mee hee woulde have put mee out of his house as a mad man & soe freinds y' was with mee stranged to see his darknesse & impatiens butt ye Lords power came over all.

And I did see he was vaine & high & proude & conceited & y' ye Lord wulde blast him & was against him & hee greived ye righteous life: & very high hee was till ye Kinge came in & afterwards hee was beheaded: but hee coulde haredly bear freindes without they woulde putt of there hatts to him (I: 314).

Indeed, a little later Vane is shown declining to try Quakers till they removed their hats (or rather till others persuaded him otherwise). Yet, though Charles II curiously concurred with Fox's view of Vane's character, the political point emerges rather cack-handedly: after all, Restoration magistrates took a very hard line with hatted Quakers appearing before them.

Fox's account of Cromwell shows how poorly even straightforward polemical strategies are accomplished within the *Journal*. The central concern seems to be to demonstrate, to the Restoration establishment, that Fox regarded Cromwell hostilely and that Quakerism suffered at his hands. Thus the *Journal* prints a letter "tenderd to ye Judges before I was praemunired" in 1673 concerning oathes, and adding:

> And I was Cast into Darby dungeon & there kept six month togeather; because I refused to take upp arrmes att Worcester fight {against Kinge Charles}: & alsoe I was carried upp as a plotter {to bringe in kinge Chalres} before Oliver Cromwell. (II: 272-73)

The fullest expression of anti-Cromwellian sentiment comes as Fox recalls the Protector's gibbeting at Tyburn and his burial beneath the gallows:

> when the Kinge came in they tooke {him} uppe & hanged him: & buryed him under Tyburn {where hee was rowled Into his grave} with Infamy.
> And when I saw him hanginge there I saw his worde Justly come upon him.
> But ye Lords power & truth spreade: & wee was promised still liberty & when it was goeinge forward one or other dirty spiritts put in papers & sett stoppe to it y^t seemd to bee for us].
> And there was about 700 freinds in prison upon contempts {to O: Cromwell: & Richarde & there goverment} when ye Kinge came in: & hee sett y^m all at liberty. (I: 385)

But the gambit cannot be sustained. Of course Charles II pretty soon set them in prison again, and on a scale and with a vindictiveness quite different from Cromwell's approach. Fox represents himself going to watch the grisly scene (even the agile turncoat Pepys, who could see the funny side of at least General Harrison's execution, found the treatment of Cromwell hard to stomach[23]). This may seem a loyalist gesture, and indeed he links his perception of it to formal praise of the king. What breaks open the polemical thrust, however, is his recollection that Cromwell really failed, not for being too revolutionary and progressive, but for not being revolutionary enough. Fox, like other radicals, regarded Cromwell at the time of the miraculous victory at Dunbar, the Cromwell who promised "hee woulde take away tyths &c" (Fox, ibid.), as a lost leader who sold out his revolutionary supporters.[24] The infamy that comes on him comes as punishment for betraying that radicalism. Fox, moreover, writes in complaint against the far stiffer measures, including his own protracted incarcerations, inflicted on the movement by a king utterly committed to a state church funded by compulsory tithing.

But then Fox's arguments of this sort are generally subverted by his persistent impulse honestly to record events as he perceived them and his own reaction to events. The *Journal* details several meetings with Cromwell in which his account of Cromwell's obvious decency towards him contrasts with his own churlishness. Thus, he buttonholes Cromwell in Hyde Park, and the Protector invites him to his home to continue the discussion, and with affable recognition of Quaker rejection of social deference sits alongside him on a table as they talk, saying "hee woulde bee as high as I was for ye Lords power came over him" – not that that wins Fox's approval (I: 259–60). What clearly emerges from the *Journal* is that Fox persistently sought to influence the Lord Protector towards. toleration of Quakerism in much the same way as he was seeking to influence Charles II, and much as he would later attempt to influence James II and perhaps William III.[25] But the text fossilizes views and attitudes and, most significantly, documents from the 1650s in the changed circumstances of the 1670s, and the result is ideological confusion and an inability to sustain a coherent political line.

Fox, however, lives comfortably with such confusion; his is a mind able to subscribe simultaneously to conflicting opinion and to hold contradictory evidence unreconciled. This is seen most vividly in his notions of providence and martyrdom. More than any other movement of the early modern period, Quakerism monitored and recorded the sufferings of its members carefully and assiduously, a practice which Fox initiated and encouraged. Indeed, the *Journal* itself peters out in lists of such sufferings, and it contains, *passim*, accounts of the painful and life-threatening experiences of Fox and others, both before and after the Restoration. Characteristically Fox frequently records the divine retribution on those that assailed him and his colleagues; that vengefulness seen in his account of the exhumation of Cromwell pervades his world vision. The pattern is set early in the *Journal*:

> I was mooved to speake to him [a certain priest] & ye people, In ye great love of God, & hee was not able to oppose, & soe they had me before ye Maior & sent mee {with some others} to ye House of Correction, but ye Iudgments of ye Lord came on y^t preist soone after & hee was cutt off & dyed. (I: 1)

The pattern recurs frequently, and always the fate of the former persecutor is linked causally to divine providence and the suffering of Fox or other Quakers: "And not longe after Judge Glyn dyed: & Major Peter Ceely & other of ye persecutinge Justices were turned out" (I: 245); "Itt was crediblely reported in y^t country y^t [a persecuting Major General's] wiffe was with childe as was thought but brought foorth a monster which they knockt it in ye heade & conveyed it secretly away" (I: 260); "And this

Judge Mallett was a cruell man & not longe after hee dyed: & Judge ffoster became a very bitter cruell man & persecuted & premunired freinds & ye Lord cutt him of alsoe: & then there came in another Lord Cheife Justice worse then ffoster for persecutinge our ffreinds & ye Lord cutt him of alsoe" (I: 384); and so on. The problem is to explain how the Lord's providence can punish persecutors while not guarding the Quakers from their wrath. If persecutors can be cut off afterwards by the Lord, why can they not be cut off at the time? Indeed, there is the added difficulty that suffering in the case of Quakers is the mark of their godliness; in the case of their enemies it is the mark of their reprobation.

The interpretative confusion is made sharper by anecdotes in which Fox rehearses examples of the Lord's special providence extended to him to a miraculous extent. In one episode Fox is cruelly beaten by a group with staffs and hedgestakes, one of them giving him a blow to his arm so bad "soe as ye people cryed out hee hath spoiled his hande for ever haveinge any use of it more," but "ye Lords power sprange through mee again & through my hande & arme y' in a minute I recovered my hande & arrme & strength" (I: 58). The Lord, so ready to refresh him, seems not to be so inclined to most of his fellow Quakers, nor indeed to be so inclined towards Fox most of the time, and all that suffering appears decidedly unprovidential.

The *Journal* defies the reading strategies which elsewhere with the prose of the mid-century prove so useful. Fox may indeed have had a case to make, may indeed have wished to have argued for a *modus vivendi* with the restored monarchy, may have sought to offer a sanitized version of Quakerism more suitable in the puritan winter of the 1660s and early 1670s. But any such tendency is unsustained. The legacy he left for his literary executors to sort out was too fissured, too contradictory, too retentive of earlier sentiments and evidence to be rendered quite coherent even by the assiduous Ellwood. Yet it documents with a directness and a detail not found in the other major autobiographies of English puritanism the complexities and confusions of its author and of the movement he served. A writer better versed in the Western literary tradition or more committed to valuing the written word rather than the spirit within would no doubt easily enough have entroped his experience within the models of martyrdom and resistance available, as Foxean witness in the manner of the *Acts and Monuments*,[26] or in the Davidic frame favored in *Eikon Basilike*. But as Penn observed, Fox is no man's copy, and the *sui generis* quality of his text, while frustrating to the critic, leaves it potent, fascinating, and raw.

NOTES

1. William Penn's Preface to the Original Edition of George Fox's Journal, 1694, in *The Journal of George Fox*, a revised edition by John L. Nickalls with an introduction by Geoffrey F. Nuttall (Cambridge: Cambridge U.P., 1952), xliii.For another view of the same passage, see below, N.H. Keeble, "The Politic and the Polite in Quaker Prose: the Case of William Penn." I am grateful to N.H. Keeble, Nigel Smith, and David Loewenstein for reading and commenting on earlier drafts of this essay.
2. Michael Philip Graves, "The Rhetoric of the Inward Light: An Examination of Extant Sermons Delivered by Early Quakers," Ph.D. dissertation, University of Southern California, 1972, 29, 33.
3. *The Journal of George Fox*, edited from the MSS by Norman Penney (1911; New York: Octagon Books, 1973), I: 27. All references are to this edition, unless otherwise stated.
4. Richard Bauman, *Let Your Words Be Few: Symbolism of Speaking and Silence among Seventeenth-Century Quakers* (Cambridge: Cambridge University Press, 1983), 126.
5. Quoted by Bauman, 126.
6. Christopher Hill, *The World Turned Upside Down: Radical Ideas During the English Revolution* (1972; Harmondsworth: Penguin, 1978), 220. On Ranter views of the limitations of language see Thomas N. Corns, *Uncloistered Virtue: English Political Literature, 1640-1660* (Oxford: Clarendon, 1992), 186–93.
7. Richard Coppin, *Divine Teachings* (London, 1649), 1–2.
8. Hill, *World*, 232.
9. The spires had been damaged in the siege of 1646, and there is some doubt how much Fox could have made out of one of them. See H. Larry Ingle, *First Among Friends: George Fox and the Creation of Quakerism* (New York and Oxford: Oxford University Press, 1994), 70 and 305, n.95.
10. Hill, *World*, 280.
11. Hill, *World*, 280.
12. Bauman, 87–9, 92. Bauman, however, attributes a greater coherence to the phenomenon than seems apparent to me. It was a practice sometimes manifested by or attributed to other radical groups, pre-eminently Ranters.
13. Friends' Library, London, manuscript volumes 376–8.
14. See, for example, T. Edmund Harvey's Introduction to Penney's edition, which is based on the Spence MS (I: xx–xxiv).
15. Penney, ed. cit., xxxiv–xxxv; Ingle, 250.
16. See, for example, Spence MS volume I: fol. 163r and 186v.
17. See Thomas N. Corns, "Bunyan's *Grace Abounding* and the Dynamics of Restoration Nonconformity," in Neil Rhodes (ed.), *History, Language, and the Politics of English Renaissance Prose* (Binghamton: MRTS, forthcoming).
18. See Thomas N. Corns, *Regaining "Paradise Lost"* (London and New York: Longman, 1994), 131–3.
19. Hill, *World*, 231; see also 256.
20. Ingle, 250–51.
21. Corns, *Uncloistered Virtue*, 90–91.
22. Ronald Hutton, *Charles II King of England, Scotland, and Ireland* (1989; Oxford and New York, Oxford University Press, 1991), 171.
23. Samuel Pepys, *The Diary of Samuel Pepys*, edited by Robert Latham and William Mathews (London: Bell, 1970), I: 265, 270, 309.
24. Christopher Hill, *God's Englishman: Oliver Cromwell and the English Revolution* (London: Weidenfeld and Nicholson, 1970), 124–5.
25. Ingle, 279, 282.
26. For a radically different view of the influence of Foxe on Fox, see John R. Knott, *Discourses of Martyrdom in English Literature, 1563-1694* (Cambridge: Cambridge University Press, 1993), chapter seven.

The Politic and the Polite in Quaker Prose: the Case of William Penn

N.H. KEEBLE

From the first moment that he came to know "pureness and righteousness" George Fox was led to associate the fidelity of Christian witness with very distinctive linguistic habits:

> for while I was a child I was taught how to walk to be kept pure. The Lord taught me to be faithful in all things, and to act faithfully two ways, viz. inwardly to God and outwardly to man, and to keep to "yea" and "nay" in all things. For the Lord showed me that though the people of the world have mouths full of deceit and changeable words, yet I was to keep to "yea" and "nay" in all things; and that my words should be few and savoury, seasoned with grace. . . .[1]

This earliest of the "openings" recorded in the *Journal* is already convinced that the Christian way with words is never careless or unthinking. Language is implicated in the fallen world and, no less than other human practices, is to be mortified and purified. To Fox, Ecclesiastes 5:2 (which he is recalling) intimated the repudiation of all merely formal courtesies and mannered protestations, of conventionally polite locutions and gestures: "the Lord . . . forbade me to put off my hat to any, high or low; and I was required to 'thee' and 'thou' all men and women, without respect to rich or poor, great or small. And as I travelled up and down, I was not to bid people 'good morrow' or 'good evening', neither might I bow or scrape with my leg to any one." The hypocrisy of the ritualistic was to be eschewed in language as in devotion or worship. Quakerism shared with all strands of Puritanism its mission "to bring people off from Jewish ceremonies, and from heathenish fables, and from men's inventions and windy doctrines," but the egalitarian radicalism of this social and linguistic nonconformity was peculiarly its own. By it Quakers intended "a fearful cut to proud flesh and self-honour," "for we saw how God would stain the world's honour and glory." In Quaker usage words were to subvert hierarchies of power and privilege by creating quite another model of human relations; they were to be tokens of neither dominance nor deference, but of integrity and trust: "I told them our allegiance did not lie in oaths but in truth and faithfulness, for they had experience enough of men's swearing first one way and then another and breaking their oaths; but our yea was our yea, and our nay was our nay."[2]

Fox was not a well educated man nor, as writer or speaker, a fluent or elegant one. In his preface to Thomas Ellwood's 1694 edition of the *Journal*, William Penn invoked 1 Corinthians 2 to turn this in a way familiar from apologies for other poorly educated Puritan writers, Bunyan for example:[3]

> And though the side of his understanding which lay next to the world, and especially the expression of it, might sound uncouth and unfashionable to nice ears, his matter was nevertheless very profound; and would not only bear to be often considered but the more it was so the more weighty and instructing it appeared. And abruptly and brokenly as sometimes his sentences would fall from him about divine things . . . it showed, beyond all contradiction, that God sent him, that no arts or parts had any share in his matter or manner of his ministry; and that so many great, excellent, and necessary truths as he came forth to preach to mankind had therefore nothing of man's wit or wisdom to recommend them; so that he was an original, being no man's copy.[4]

The extent to which Fox was unfashionable, the degree to which his language grated on "nice ears," was for Penn both a measure of his integrity and evidence of the inspired nature of his message. This had been the thrust of Penn's own most substantial work, *No Cross, No Crown*. As originally written in the Tower within two years of Penn's convincement, and published in 1669, this was a tract of fairly modest scope presenting, in the words of its title-page, *Several Sober Reasons against Hat-Honour, Titular-Respects, You to a Single Person, with the Apparel and Recreation of the Times*. In its greatly enlarged second edition (1682) a far more thorough-going renunciation of the ways of the world in general, and of the ways of London society in particular, was urged. Though "Sumptuous apparel, rich unguents, delicate washes, stately furniture, costly cookery, and such diversions as balls, masques, music-meetings, plays, romances, &c. . . . are the delights and entertainment of the times," these "belong not to the holy path that Jesus and his true disciples and followers trod to glory." The courtly and cavalier in Restoration culture is excoriated for its self-indulgence and hedonistic excess, and for its superficiality and sycophancy: "men become acceptable by their trims and the a-la-modeness of their dress and apparel . . . nothing being more notorious than the cringing, scraping, sirring, and madaming of persons, according to the gaudiness of their attire." "Gaudy superfluity" is the mark of a society which values "gold, and silver, ribbons, laces, prints, perfumes, costly clothes, curious trims, exact dresses, rich jewels, romances, love-songs, and the like pastimes." By contrast, "Abraham, Isaac and Jacob were plain men"; Jesus was "in life of great plainness." In place of preoccupation with "shops, exchanges, plays, parks, coffee-houses, &c.," "curiosity, pomp, exchange of apparel, honours, preferments, fashions, and the customary recreations of the world," Penn offers an ideal "of temperance, and some good and beneficial end."[5]

Since this ideal may be realised "more or less . . . in every action,"[6] abstinence and utility are to be sought in writing as in all other human endeavors. These criteria determine what may be the earliest sustained account of Quaker literary principles,[7] Penn's characterization of Quaker style in his preface to *The Written Gospel Labours of John Whitehead* (1704):

> *[the reader] is not to expect the Learning of the* Schools, *unless it be of the* Prophets, *and of the* Enlightened *and* Spiritual Generations *of Men; and of a plain, sound and practical Knowledge, to be felt . . . evidently by those that are in any Measure restored to the Exercise of their* Spiritual Senses. . . . *Neither . . . hath this Godly Author labour'd a nice or polish'd Stile, which Men usually do, to give a Lustre to, or Varnish their Matter with, but writes as an* Enlightened *and* Experienced *Man.*[8]

It is in these terms that Penn characteristically refers to his own literary manner: "I desire to open my Mind, both with Tenderness and Plainness."[9] He associated this stylistic quality of "plainness" both with the integrity of that "Plain Dealing" which becomes the character of a friend to truth,[10] and with direct and immediate communication:

> *I have endeavoured to express my self in* Plain *and* Proper *Terms, and not* Figurative, Allegorical *or* Doubtful *Phrases; that so I may leave* no room *for an* Equivocal or Double Sence; *but that the* Truth *of the Subject I treat upon, may appear* Easily *and* Evidently *to every common Understanding.*[11]

If plainness marks straightforward dealing in the truth then linguistic dexterity is the subterfuge of hypocrisy and wilful obfuscation. In perhaps his most popular work, the apophthegmatic collection *Some Fruits of Solitude* (1693), Penn is very wary of stylistic elaboration. He allows that "There is a truth and beauty in rhetoric," but, he goes on, "it oftener serves ill turns than good ones"; stylistic elegance "has a moving grace," but "it is too artificial for simplicity and oftentimes for truth." "Affect not words but matter," he advises his children, "and chiefly to be pertinent and plain; truest eloquence is plainest."[12]

It is again 1 Corinthians 2 which lies behind these remarks, as it does behind any number of Puritan pronouncements upon the desirability of plainness in prose style. Quaker plainness is not, however, Puritan plainness. For an early Quaker to write as "an Enlightened and Experienced Man" was to produce something far more rhapsodical, figurative and allusive, something altogether more unbuttoned and unpredictable, than would satisfy the scrupulous desire for accurate exposition of a Baxter.[13] Exclusive concentration upon the integrity of the self and the immediate experience of the Spirit could lead to intensely subjective, non-referential writing[14] which, in the view of a Bunyan, was disqualified precisely by its weak grip on material fact.[15] For all his advocacy of plainness, such Puritan critics might easily have found in Penn himself examples of the "Figurative, Allegorical *or* Doubtful *Phrases*" they so disliked. In his first Quaker publication, an impassioned eighteen-page tract which addresses "ye Idolatrous, Superstitious, Carnal, Proud, Wanton, Unclean, Mocking and Persecuting *Princes, Priests* and *People*" with all the confidence of the new convert whom, says the title-page, *Divine Love constrains in a holy contempt to trample on Egypt's glory, not fearing the King's wrath, having beheld the Majesty of him who is Invisible*, Penn lambasts the failings of "ye dark and Idolatrous *Papists*, ye superstitious and loose *Protestants*" in an interrogative and exclamatory cascade which cannot stay for syntactical niceties.[16] And on occasions throughout his career Penn wrote in this hortatory and admonitory manner. It is a style incantatory, repetitive, evocative, a style in which to enthuse but not to argue, a manner so rapt that the self may become one with the divine. Penn unhesitatingly adopts the first person to pronounce God's apocalyptic judgments in an unpublished 1670 piece, "God's Controversy Proclaimed to the Nation":

> Hear and harken unto these things, o ye Inhabitants of this Isle, for I the Lord have thundred out of Sion, & my powerfull Word is gone forth from Jerusalem, tremble you that hear these things, & let your Lipps quiver at the Voyce thereof, that you may all rest in the day of trouble; for a Day of sorrow, & a Day of Anguish, a Day of howling, & a Day of gnashing of Teeth is coming upon the Nations: And the time of Baylons, that Harlot, that false Church, that sayes, she is the Lambs Wife, & is not, but full of Abominations, being judged, her Bratts will I dash against the stones, her glory will I stayn, her pride will I lay in the dust, & her Cruelty will I recompence upon her head, she shal be a stinck amongst the People, & her Name shall be an hissing among the Nations; & the beastly power will I destroy, & the fals hireling prophet will I smite, & the Dragon that old Serpent will I overcome. . . .[17]

He who speaks in the voice of God has few qualms. The uncritical confidence with which this passage makes free with Biblical texts is oblivious to incongruity or indecorum; it is a style in which irony and moderation are alike impossible.

It is also a style available to the untutored, a style which enables and authorizes the utterance of people without access to university, court and town, and with no knowledge of polite conventions of taste and decorum. The appeal of seventeenth-century Quakerism was predominantly to those beyond the pale of courtly and gentle codes, to traders, artisans, agricultural workers and labourers. Empowered by their Quaker conviction they were no longer disqualified from authorship. In *No Cross, No Crown* it was, after all, to the "generally poor" prophets, the apostles who were "poor men," and Jesus who "was of poor descent" that Penn looked for an ideal preferable to that of the London *beau monde*.[18] Penn himself, however, was certainly not untutored, nor disadvantaged, nor marginalised. By birth and upbringing he was a member of that élite whose ways *No Cross, No Crown* so uncompromisingly rejected. The son of a father knighted at the Restoration and high in the favor of Charles II, a former student of Oxford and of the Inns of Court, a fine swordsman who returned from his Grand Tour looking, in the opinion of Elizabeth Pepys, "a most modish person . . . a fine gentleman," though in Samuel Pepys's view having "a great deal, if not too much, of the vanity of the French garbe and affected manner of speech and gait,"[19] this man had no need of empowerment.[20] On the contrary, for him to choose Quakerism appeared to be a peculiarly perverse repudiation of all to which he was entitled. On the occasion of his arrest in 1671 Sir John Robinson, Governor of the Tower, remarked in bewilderment at Penn's social disgrace:

> I vow Mr. Penn I am sorry for you, you are an Ingenious Gentleman, all the World must allow you, & do allow you that, & you have a plentifull Estate, why should you render your self unhappy by associating with such a simple People.[21]

The affront caused to his peers by a commitment which landed him in the Tower is alluded to in the prefatory epistle to the 1669 edition of *No Cross, No Crown*. Addressing "my Ancient Friends,"[22] Penn presents the text as an answer to "the Objections with which you have frequently beset me." Something of the nature of these objections may be surmised from Pepys's being told in December 1667 that Penn "is a Quaker again, or some very melancholy thing; that he cares for no company, nor comes into any."[23] The book sets out to justify a course of life which to aspiring young professional men and to town gallants appeared at best dull and tedious, at worst nonsensical and outrageous in its flouting of gentlemanly behavior. It seeks also to incite those "ancient friends" to relinquish *"that vanity of vanities*; I mean, those Fashions, Pleasures, and that whole variety of Conversation which make up the Life and satisfaction of the Age."[24] Of Penn himself, however, Quakerism demanded not that he turn his back on the "whole variety of [London] Conversation," its politics, patronage and culture, but rather that he use his privileged position to Quaker advantage. The fascination of his biography resides in the way that, for the rest of his career, he negotiated apparently incompatible positions: Quaker and courtier, quietist and politician, radical dissenter and governor and proprietor of Pennsylvania, libertarian Whig and supporter of James II.[25] Looking back in an unpublished autobiographical paper written probably in the 1690s Penn himself speaks of "findeing my self narrowed in this manner, that one day I was received well at court as Prop[rietor] & Go[vernor] of a province of the Crown, & the next taken up at a meeting by [the informers] hilton or collingwood, & the third smoakt & informed of for meeting with men of the whig stamp."[26] Such an habitué of two worlds has need to be master of the discourse of two worlds. And so Penn was. In his political tracts – the larger part of the body of his writings – he bears himself not as the simple enthusiast who so perplexed Robinson but in a cultivated manner his "ancient friends" would, immediately and approvingly, have recognised.

In the first place, the tracts against persecution in the 1670s and 1680s, the pieces associated with the Exclusion Crisis of 1679–81, and the pamphlets in support of James II's policy of Indulgence and for repeal of the penal laws and Test Acts, all keep very quiet about Quakerism. Their usually anonymous author is characterized not in religious, and certainly not in sectarian, but in national terms. "Thus have I honestly and plainly clear'd my Conscience for my *Country*" Penn concludes one anonymous tract, signing himself "An *English-Christian-Man*." Another, written on behalf of "We, the *Commons of England*," is signed "England's *True Friend*, PHILANGLUS."[27] "*No matter* who, *but* what," says Penn of the anonymity of a third tract; "*and yet if thou wouldst know the Author , he is an* English-man, and *therefore obliged to this Country, and the Laws that made him Free.*"[28]

In such cases, Penn is not, as might be supposed, simply availing himself of that anonymity so frequently adopted by dissident writers (and especially Quakers) during the Restoration period in order to avoid the penalties of illegal publication.[29] Anonymity is assumed as a matter of rhetorical decorum as much as of self-interest. Published in 1687 on behalf of the royal policy of toleration, the anonymous *Good Advice to the Church of England* was licensed; thus sanctioned, its publication was quite legal and its author at no risk. What was at risk, however, was the reception of his argument by the polite readers Penn had in mind. Polemical prudence dictates that Penn should withhold his identity. To associate his case, through his name, with the despised and vulgar (and probably seditious) practices of the Quakers would be to disable it all but fatally. Rather, Penn presents himself, as he had done in the famous trial which resulted in Bushel's Case, reported in *The People's Antient and Just Liberties Asserted* (1670),[30] as a patriotic Englishman, convinced, in the Whig way, of the antiquity of the English constitution, of "our undoubted Birthright of English Freedoms," and that "*our own good, old, admirable* Laws *of* England, *have made such excellent provision for its* inhabitants" that, were they but applied, tyranny and persecution would cease. He defends not a sect but "*the* Lives, Liberties, *and* Properties *of so many thousand free-born English Families.*[31]

This free-born Englishman is of gentle birth and well educated. Both Classical learning and the later European tradition are at his disposal. This is so even in Penn's overtly Quaker pieces: the second part of *No Cross, No Crown*, a third of the book, is given over to the "Testimonies of several Great, Learned and Virtuous Personages." In a letter of 1693 to Sir John Rodes, "probably the highest-born Quaker of his generation," Penn saw no impropriety in giving directions for "a moderate library" of some one hundred titles covering all disciplines. He gave besides advice on marginal annotation and the use of pocket and commonplace books "to fasten *what* one reads and to be master of other mens sense."[32] Penn was certainly the master of the "sense" of a good many "other men" and frequently adduces it to strengthen his argument. In the political tracts, there are explicitly three courts of appeal: *The Great Case of Liberty of Conscience* is urged, in the words of its title-page, *by the authority of reason, scripture and antiquity*. Its argument is sustained by citations from such Classical writers as Cato, Livy and Tacitus, from Eusebius and the Church Fathers, from "honest *Chaucer*, whose Matter (not his Poetry) heartely affects me," from the "Famous *Raleigh*" and from "*Doctor Hammond* himself, the *Grand Patron of the English Church.*"[33] Elsewhere, that "witty man" Cowley and "that extraordinary Man *J. Hales* of *Eton*'[34] are adduced.

Penn does not rely upon mere citation. He can apply his "humane" authorities with some deftness. The tricky business of commending the case of the suffering nonconformists, for example, is managed by avoiding any appeal to the religious grounds his episcopalian readership would contest. Instead, Penn refers to a Classical precedent his readers have been taught to accept as exemplary:

> *And we are bold to say, the grand* Fomentors *of Persecution, are no better Friends to the English State, then were* Anytus *and*

Aristophanes *of old to that of* Athens, *the Case being somewhat the same, as that they did not more bitterly envy the Reputation of* Socrates *amongst* the Athenians for his grave and religious lectures (*thereby giving the* Youth *a diversion from frequenting their* Plays) *then some now emulate the true* Dissenter, *for his Pious Life, and great Industry.*[35]

This is to situate the nonconformists in a rational, moral and moderate tradition far removed from the irrational enthusiasm attributed to them by such Tory pamphleteers as Sir Roger L'Estrange. It is a neat piece of polemical strategy, wrong-footing his opponents. Like them, Penn posits a commonwealth of rationality and commonsense, as well as of faith, but he reverses their allocation of roles:

The Understanding can never be convinc'd, nor properly submit, but by such Arguments, as are *Rational, Perswasive and Sutable to its own Nature* . . . but to imagine those *Barbarous Newgate Instruments of* Clubbs, Fines, Prisons &c. . . . *should be fit Arguments to convince the* Understanding . . . is altogether irrational, cruel, impossible.[36]

Irrationality and barbarism belong not to the dissenters but to the persecutors. For his opponents to advocate persecution is thus for them to betray the very culture they espouse.

The learning so effectively deployed is carried not with the pedantry of the scholar but with the ease of a man of the world well-versed in current affairs. Arguing that toleration does not jeopardise the security of the state Penn is able to give contemporary "forreign instances" and to adduce European history and historians from Caesar to Spelman, with something of a lawyer's concern for precedents.[37] If the result is an accumulation of cases rather than a critical analysis of causation or developments, that is because Penn is seeking witnesses to testify, not theorizing about history.[38] The persuasiveness of one of his most highly regarded and most frequently reprinted tracts, *An Essay towards the Present and Future Peace of Europe by the Establishment of an European Dyet, Parliament or Estates* (1693), derives largely from its being not a work of political theory but the product of experience. Its advocate is one who has "made the great tour of Europe," who knows the problems of passport controls and who recommends that proceedings in any European parliament should be in French since that is "most easy for men of quality".[39] It is a curious irony that this tract concerned wholly with political realities, should, in one sense, have proved the most prophetic of all Penn's works.

The *Essay* has no very high expectations of politicians. It confines itself to the politically possible on the grounds of the politically expedient.

Though committed to liberal, even idealistic, causes, Penn's political tracts recognise the imperatives of a markedly secular world. Mary Maples Dunn has remarked the increasing incidence of argument from interest, rather than principle, in the later pamphlets.[40] Penn's promotional pieces on behalf of settlement in Pennsylvania understandably appeal to people's material interests, but so, too, do the arguments for toleration, pointing to the stability of the nation and the benefit to trade. On occasions, they can assume an almost Hobbesian hardheadedness:

> Nothing, humanely speaking, fixes any Man like his Interest; And tho this Agreement [to accept James's Indulgence] were only *Hobson*'s choice in *Roman Catholick* and *Dissenter*, the security is not the less: For whatever be the Morality of any Party, if I am sure of them by the side of *Interest* and *Necessity*, I will never seek or value an *Ensurance* by Oath and Tests. *Interest* is the choice Men naturally make.[41]

Penn here speaks in accents very like the Machiavellian tones of Marchamont Needham in, for example, *Interest Will Not Lie* (1660).[42] He has become, if not a pragmatist and temporizer, one who has at least to explain that he is not a pragmatist and temporizer, as he does in a passage in *Good Advice* when, noting that " 'tis the Wisdom of a Man to *observe* the Courses, and *humor* the Motions of his Interest," he adds that he means only the *moral* pursuit of his interest and not any "immoral or corrupt complyance: A *Temporizing*, deservedly base with Men of Vertue."[43]

He may side with the men of virtue but men of the world are wary of dogmatic distinctions and, in his political writings, Penn is sensitive to their suspicions of absolute commitment as both imprudent and rather vulgar. He comports himself with none of a Quaker's intensity. On the contrary, he is genial and good-tempered. The opening page of *Good Advice* is an exercise in urbane discourse which has far more in common with Halifax than with Fox. Penn presents himself as a disinterested public servant, one concerned but far from fanatical, one committed to principle but above party or sectarian allegiance:

> I must own, it is my Aversion at this time, to meddle with Publick Matters, and yet my Duty to the Publick will not let me be Silent. They that move by Principles must not regard *Times* nor *Factions*, but what is *just*, and what is *honourable*; and that no Man ought to Scruple, nor no Time nor Interest to Contest.

This apparent disinclination to become involved is far from the Quaker's headlong readiness to obtrude himself discordantly into any discussion or occasion. It situates the authorial persona in quite another tradition. His poise is in a line which reaches both back to Sir Philip Sidney and the Italian ideal of *sprezzatura* and forward to a Lockean age of reason and common sense. In the place of the assertiveness of Quaker discourse we are offered a considered exchange in which the writer "humbly submit[s] my Reasons to every reasonable Conscience." Indeed, he is so very reasonable, he can entertain the possibility he is in error, but "if I am mistaken, it is with so great an inclination to serve them all [the Church of England, Roman Catholics and dissenters], that their good nature cannot but plead my Excuse." No Quaker ever allowed "good nature" to the hireling priests of the established English or Roman churches. Here, however, there are no such categorical distinctions to be made between sheep and goats, no charges of hypocrisy, self-interest, cruelty. When a gentleman writes *A Letter from a Gentleman in the Country to his Friends in London, upon the subject of the penal laws and tests* (1687) we are in the company of people civil and civilised, without malice, without passion. The worst offence that can be committed, on either side, is to be mistaken.

There are times when Penn grows more heated, but when he does it is with the heat of "that grand Whig Milton,"[44] the Milton of the anti-prelatical tracts, rather than with the fervour of a Nayler or a Penington. The Church of England, he argues, like the Roman Church, is interested in power, "*to keep all to herself*"; her opposition to toleration stems from fear that she will lose "that Power the Law gives her to domineer over all Dissenters,"

> And is not this a *Rare Motive* for a Christian Church to continue Penal Law for Religion? If her Piety be not able to maintain her upon equal terms, methinks her having so much the whip hand and start of all others, should satisfy her Ambition, and quiet her Fears. . . . She might perswade and convince what she could: And pray, is not that enough for a true Church, without *Goales, Whips, Halters* and *Gibbets*? O what corruption is this that has prevail'd over Men of such Pretensions to Light and Conscience? that they do not, or will not, see nor feel their own Principles one remove from themselves; but sacrifice the noblest part of the Reformation to Ambition, and compel Men to truckle their tender consciences to the Grandure and Dominion of their Doctors.[45]

There is not only Milton's heat and anticlericalism but, in the last sentence, something also of his rhythmical and alliterative force and his trick of disturbing the register with a sudden colloquialism.

More usually, though, Penn's sustained periods advance his points with great circumspection, steadily accumulating evidence and answering objections till their conclusions emerge with quiet inevitability:

> If the *Consequences* that are imagin'd to follow the *Repeal* of the *Penal Statutes* and *Tests* (and which so many give for the reason of their dislike to the Liberty that is sought by it) were indeed so *Terrible* as they are industriously represented, I should readily fall in with the common Jealousie, and help to augment the number of those that are for *their* Continuance; but when I consider how long our Government was *Happy* without *Them*, how much of *heat* and *partiality* prevail'd in their Constitution, and how *troublesome* and *impracticable* their Execution are, and that, in our present Circumstances, *They* appear a plain *Barriere* to our Happiness, instead of a *Bulwark* to our Religion, I cannot but lament the misfortune of the *Publick*, that those Gentlemen are yet under the fatal mistake of thinking Them necessary to our Safety, that with more Reason and Charity, in my opinion, should *Endeavour to save us* from the Inconveniences of them.[46]

We are again dealing with the *mistakes* of *gentlemen*, and gentlemanly mistakes require judicious and tactful refutation, not castigation or denunciation. It is not a divine oracle but *my opinion* that is put forward, with the tentativeness proper (in this discourse) to the personal and the deference due to one's peers. Rather than antagonize, Penn mollifies. Commending liberty of conscience to Parliament he is sufficiently politic to acknowledge that "'tis the infelicity of Governors to see and hear by the *Eyes* and *Ears* of other men," and so "We would not attribute the whole of this severity [of persecution] to *Malice*, since not a little share, may justly be ascrib'd to *Mis-intelligence*."[47] When he is sharper, it is with the pointedness of wit, rather than the force of moral indignation: "Things don't change, tho men do"; "To be a *True* Church is better then to be a *National* one."[48] As such terse summary aphorisms intimate, his suspicion of fulsome rhetoric is as much Neo-classical as Puritan. Pope's *Essay on Criticism* is not far away when we read, among the dicta on *wit* in *Fruits of Solitude*: "Less judgement than wit is more sail than ballast"; "Where judgment has wit to express it, there's the best orator."[49] Similarly, the genres he takes up – the topical essay, the letter from the country, advice to children, the "enchiridion', as he calls *Fruits of Solitude* in its preface – are those of cultivated discourse, measured and reasonable. Both they and Quaker writing come freighted with experience: but the experience of the one is shared, public and reassuring; of the other subjective, private, subversive.

What this paper has described is a literary temper of the last quarter of the seventeenth century, a temper shaped and sustained, if not determined, by a combination of personal, religious, social and cultural factors. When, in 1673, the Second-day's Morning Meeting was set up to oversee and supervise Quaker publication, Penn was appointed a member. It was the business of the Meeting to ensure that nothing went into print which misrepresented the Quaker position and that all anti-Quaker publications were answered.[50] In an important article[51] Thomas O'Malley has argued that in practice this control of the Quaker press ensured that "the sort of aggressive prophetic material that had been produced in the 1650s" did not continue to appear in the 1670s and 1680s, and that only works which might obtain relief from (rather than exacerbate) persecution should appear. Penn's own literary manner belongs to this more cautious context and, to a degree, it may be understood as part of a deliberate policy to modify the public image of Quakerism; but his writing is a product also of Penn's own age, class and upbringing. Born in 1644 and convinced in 1667, he was of the second generation of Quakers, shaped less by radical expectancy than by persecution and the need to survive. He set his face against all that "Restoration" commonly signifies culturally, but, well-educated, schooled in the ways of a social élite and reaching maturity in the 1660s, he was susceptible to its taste and sensitive to its manners as Fox never was. And, finally, Penn's rhetorical strategy was the product of polemical prudence, the creation of a skilled pamphleteer. To have recommended the Quaker case in Quaker language to the political and religious establishment would have been to disqualify it by inviting ridicule and obloquy. The case required a style still plain but capable of lucid exposition and of handling evidence; a style reassuringly reasonable yet engagé; the style not of Quakers but of Whigs, trimmers and latitudinarians; a literary temporizing demanded, perhaps, by *interest*.

NOTES

1. George Fox, *The Journal*, ed. John L. Nickalls (London: Religious Society of Friends, 1975), 1–2.
2. Fox, 36, 242, 416, 463.
3. See the prefaces by John Burton and John Gibbs to Bunyan's earliest publications, *Some Gospel-Truths Opened* (1656) and *A Few Sighs from Hell* (1658), in vol. 1 of *Miscellaneous Works*, ed. T.L. Underwood and Roger Sharrock (Oxford: Clarendon Press, 1980), 12, 244.
4. Fox, p. xliii.
5. William Penn, *No Cross, No Crown*, ed. Norman Penney (1930; reprint, York: William Sessions, 1981), 213, 219, 222, 223, 229-30, 233, 244–5, 246. For discussions of this work and its place in the culture of later Puritanism see N.H. Keeble, *The Literary Culture of Nonconformity in Later Seventeenth-century England* (Leicester: Leicester University Press 1987), chapter 7.
6. Penn, *No Cross, No Crown*, 233.
7. It is so regarded by Luella M. Wright, *The Literary Life of the Early Friends, 1650–1725*

(New York: Columbia University Press, 1932), 57–73.

8. W[illiam] P[enn], preface to *The Written Gospel Labours of John Whitehead* (London, 1704), sig. A3.

9. W[illiam] P[enn], *Just Measures, in an Epistle of Peace and Love*, 2nd ed. ad cal with *A Brief Examination and State of Liberty Spiritual* (London, [1695?]; 90B; P1260A), 28. (Penn's tracts were printed and reprinted in various states, often in the same year. To identify the issue cited, the yeardate is followed by the number allocated both in E.B. Bronner and David Fraser, *William Penn's Published Writings, 1660–1726: An Interpretive Bibliography*, vol. 5 of R.S. and Mary Maples Dunn, eds., *The Papers of William Penn* [Philadelphia, PA: University of Pennsylvania Press, 1986] and in Wing.)

10. [William Penn], *Good Advice to the Church of England, Roman Catholick, and Protestant Dissenter*, 2nd ed. ([London], 1687; 82B P1296A), 13.

11. William Penn, *Primitive Christianity Revived in the Faith and Practice of the People called Quakers* (London, 1696; 104A; P1342), sigs. B2v – B3r.

12. William Penn, *Some Fruits of Solitude* (1693) and *Fruits of a Father's Love* (1726) in *The Peace of Europe: The Fruits of Solitude, and other writings*, Everyman's Library (London: Dent, n.d.), 41. 102 (hereafter cited as *EL*).

13. See N.H. Keeble, *Richard Baxter: Puritan Man of Letters* (Oxford: Clarendon Press, 1982), 62–8.

14. For a description of this style see Jackson I. Cope, "Seventeenth-Century Quaker Style," in *Seventeenth-Century Prose Style*, ed. Stanley Fish (New York: Oxford University Press, 1971), 200-35. For its sources, analogues and context, see Nigel Smith, *Perfection Proclaimed: Language and Literature in English Radical Religion, 1640–1660* (Oxford: Clarendon Press, 1989).

15. John Bunyan, *Some Gospel-Truths Opened* (London, 1656) in vol. 1 of *Miscellaneous Works*, esp. 79–80, 114–15.

16. William Penn, *Truth Exalted in a Short, but Sure, Testimony against All those Religions, Faiths, and Worships that Have Been Formed and Followed in the Darkness of Apostacy* (London, 1668; 2A; P1389), 16, 17.

17. R.S. and Mary Maples Dunn, eds., *The Papers of William Penn* (Philadelphia, PA: University of Pennsylvania Press, 1981), 1:187.

18. Penn, *No Cross, No Crown*, 222, 223, 224.

19. Robert Latham and William Matthews, eds., *The Diary of Samuel Pepys* (1971; reprint, London: Bell, 1974), 5:255, 257 (26 & 30 August 1664).

20. For Penn's biography, see William I. Hull, *William Penn: A Topical Biography* (London: Oxford University Press, 1937); William Comfort, *The Life of William Penn* (Philadelphia: University of Pennsylvania Press, 1944); Catherine Owens Peare, *William Penn: A Biography* (London: Dobson, 1956).

21. *Papers of Penn*, 1:199.

22. These eight friends, identified in the text only by their initials, may have included Henry Sidney, the brother of Algernon Sidney on whose behalf Penn would afterwards campaign in the 1679 elections, and Isaac Newton (William C. Braithwaite, *The Second Period of Quakerism*, 2nd ed. (1961; reprint York: William Sessions, 1979), 62n; Hugh Barbour, foreword to Penn, *No Cross, No Crown*, xxiii, n2).

23. *Diary of Pepys*, vol. 8 (1974; reprint, London: Bell, 1975), 595 (29 December 1667).

24. W[illiam] Penn, *No Cross, No Crown*, ([London], 1669; 6; P1327), sigs. A2r – A2v.

25. For this tension, and for Penn's political career in general, see: Vincent Buranelli, *The King and the Quaker* (Philadelphia, PA: University of Pennsylvania Press, 1962); Joseph E. Illick, *William Penn the Politician: His Relations with the English Government* (Ithaca, NY: Cornell University Press, 1965); Mary Maples Dunn, *William Penn: Politics and Conscience* (Princeton, NJ: Princeton University Press, 1967); Richard S. Dunn, "William Penn's Odyssey: From Child of Light to Absentee Landlord," in *Public Duty and Private Conscience in Seventeenth-Century England: Essays Presented to G.E. Aylmer*, ed. John Morrill, Paul Slack and Daniel Woolf (Oxford: Clarendon Press, 1993), 305–25.

26. *Papers of Penn*, vol. 3 (Philadelphia, PA: University of Pennsylvania Press, 1986), 342.

27. [William Penn], *England's Present Interest Discover'd with Honour to the Prince and Safety*

to the People ([London], 1675; 39A; P1279), 27, 28 [recte 59, 60]; [William Penn], *England's Great Interest in the Choice of this New Parliament* ([London, 1679]; 50A; P1278), 2, 4.

28. [Penn], *Good Advice*, sig. A1.
29. For censorship as it affected nonconformist writing, and the uses of anonymity to combat it, see Keeble, *Literary Culture*, chapter 3, esp. 111–13.
30. Keeble, *Literary Culture*, 52, 86–7.
31. W[illiam] P[enn], *The Great Case of Liberty of Conscience Once More Briefly Debated & Defended*, 2nd ed. ([London], 1670[/1]; 9B; P1299var), 4, 6.
32. *Papers of Penn*, 3:378–9.
33. [Penn], *The Great Case*, 39–42.
34. *EL*, 104; William Penn, *An Address to Protestants upon the Present Conjuncture*, 2nd ed. ([London], 1679; 48C; P1248), 120, 157, 172.
35. [Penn], *The Great Case*, 5. Anytus was one of the prosecutors at Socrates's trial; Aristophanes ridiculed Socrates in his comedy *The Clouds*.
36. [Penn], *The Great Case*, 21.
37. [William Penn], *A Perswasive of Moderation to Church Dissenters* ([London, 1686?]; var. of 72C; P1338A), *passim*.
38. This point is made in Dunn, *William Penn*, 48–50.
39. *EL*, 12, 17.
40. Dunn, *William Penn*, 134–5.
41. [William Penn], *The Great and Popular Objection against the Repeal of the Penal Laws and Tests Briefly Stated and Consider'd* (London, 1688; 83A; P1298A), 15–16.
42. I am indebted to Thomas Corns for this observation.
43. [Penn], *Good Advice*, 37 (quoted by Dunn, *William Penn*, 135).
44. Cf. George Sensabaugh, *That Grand Whig Milton* (Stanford, CA: Stanford University Press, 1952).
45. [Penn], *Good Advice*, 8, 9.
46. [Penn], *The Great and Popular Objection*, 3–4.
47. [Penn], *The Great Case*, pref. ep. [p. 1v].
48. [Penn], *Good Advice*, 14, 18.
49. *EL*, 43.
50. On the establishment and work of this committee see Braithwaite, 279-81; Wright, 97–109.
51. Thomas O'Malley, "'Defying the Powers and Tempering the Spirit': A Review of Quaker Control over their Publications, 1672–1689", *Journal of Ecclesiastical History* 33, no. 1 (1982): 72-88. See also Cope, 223–7.

Joseph Besse and the Quaker Culture of Suffering

JOHN R. KNOTT

In his excellent study of the interactions of Quakers with the legal system in the period of the greatest persecution (1660–88), Craig Horle complains about the tendency of Quaker historians to perpetuate the image of Quakers joyfully suffering hardships at the hands of cruel persecutors.[1] According to his revisionist argument, the persecutions were not as severe and the suffering not as passive as the received view of the early Quakers would have us believe. Horle effectively complicates the picture of Quaker suffering by examining in detail how the penal laws were used against them in a pattern of enforcement he finds "sporadic and capricious" and by demonstrating the growing sophistication of Quakers in pursuing legal means of resistance. While he recognizes and describes the violence against Quakers in the period, Horle focusses on Quaker activism in gathering and publishing their "sufferings" as a way of confronting their persecutors and judges and in developing a legal support system through the Meeting for Sufferings, established in London in 1676.

My own interest, as literary historian, is in the story of suffering the Quakers told, particularly as this emerges from the retrospective *Collection of the Sufferings of the People Called Quakers* (1753) that Joseph Besse compiled from the reports of sufferings sent to London and collected in the manuscript Great Book of Sufferings by Ellis Hookes and from other "Authentick Accounts," presumably the numerous published accounts of particular sufferings. This story needs to be understood in relation to the context established by Horle and other recent commentators on the radical social and political culture of the late seventeenth century,[2] but it is interesting in itself for what it reveals about the ways Quakers understood and presented the persecution and suffering that contributed so significantly to their self-definition and to the growth of their movement.

Besse's two folio volumes offer an overview of the persecution of Quakers in the period up to the Toleration Act (1650–89) from the perspective of someone looking back at what had come to be seen as the heroic age of Quakerism.[3] As I have suggested elsewhere, Besse's *Sufferings* constitutes a Quaker Book of Martyrs, influenced by John Foxe's *Acts and Monuments* in its thematic emphases and in the practice of reproducing original documents (including the texts of Acts, warrants, petitions for relief, and accounts of examinations and trials in Besse's case).[4] Besse like Foxe, albeit for a much shorter time period, relies on the accumulation of detail to convey the enormity of the persecution suffered by the faithful and the magnitude of their spiritual victory. His method of proceeding chronologically through each county and also the countries and colonies to which the Quakers sent missions (in Europe and the New World) makes his narrrative seem even more exhaustive than Foxe's. Yet this impression of completeness is misleading, since Besse's multiple narratives do not reproduce all the incidents in his sources, which themselves do not capture all the incidents that might qualify as "sufferings," or their fullness of detail.[5]

In reading Besse one must remember that his sensibility was shaped by the nature of the Quakerism that had evolved by the time he wrote: stabler, quieter, more rational, and more concerned with decorum than that of the period he chronicled. Like others who described this period or edited the works of its leading figures (Thomas Ellwood editing George Fox's *Journal*, for example), he was capable of omitting what had come to seem extravagances of language or behavior. Where the early Quakers talk about responding to the leadings of the Spirit, Besse is likelier to speak of duty: "they experienced an inward Peace and Tranquillity of Mind, strengthening and enabling them to persevere in the *Way* of their *Duty*."[6] His voice tends to be pious and moderate, considerably removed from the prophetic urgency of many of the early Quaker tracts and from the polemical zeal of John Foxe as well. Yet one should not make *too* much of the shift in sensibility one finds in Besse. If the tone and some of the emphases have changed, the outlines of the story and the understanding of the character and significance of Quaker suffering have not. And Besse amply registers his compassion for the victims of persecution, especially the more vulnerable, and expresses his outrage at the violations they suffered, often through the detail he chooses to record ("In like manner did they abuse others of the Assembly, pulling off the Womens Headclothes and daubing their Faces with Filth and Excrements" [1:87]). Occasionally the voice breaks, as when he interrupts an account of the abuses of Quakers by Oxford students who interrupted a Quaker meeting: "I am weary of transcribing their Abominations" (1:566). One encounters many other voices in the materials reproduced by Besse, of course, some in their prophetic urgency or their anticipations of divine vengeance clashing with his own.

The larger story of the triumph of the Quakers over their enemies was firmly established by the time Besse wrote. In *A Brief Account of the Rise and Progress of the People Called Quakers*, published in 1694 as an introduction to the first edition of George Fox's *Journal*, William Penn described the growth of a movement based in a kind of "Truth-speaking" that inevitably called forth calumny and persecution. He reinforced the image of the Quakers as a suffering people who revived the spirit of primitive Christianity: "they came forth *low* and *despised*, and *hated*, as the Primitive Christians did."[7] Penn insisted that the Quakers were peaceable ("*Not Fighting*, but *Suffering*"), obedient to civil magistrates, and inclined to forgive their enemies rather than seek revenge. The Peace Testimony had become an integral part of Quaker life by this time.[8] It was important for Penn to establish the posture with which Quakers endured persecution as well as the fact of their suffering. Thus he emphasized their "great Constancy and Patience in suffering for their Testimony . . . and that sometimes unto *Death*, by *Beatings*, *Bruisings*, long and crouded *Imprisonments*, and noisome *Dungeons*." Such a characterization clearly aligned the Quakers' experience of persecution with the tradition of Christian martyrology, adapted to English protestantism by John Foxe. Where Foxe associated the suffering of his martyrs primarily with the scene of execution, however, Penn and subsequent chroniclers represent Quaker suffering as virtually continuous. The lives they describe appear suffused with the spirit of martyrdom, provoking ever more furious reactions, which in turn call for ever greater displays of patience.

The first important history of the Quakers, William Sewel's *The History of the People Called Quakers* (1722),[9] tells a story of progress through suffering similar to Penn's, although with greater emphasis on the heroic character of Quaker endurance. Quaker prisoners in Bristol, Sewel reports, "continued now so valiant, and without fainting, that some of their persecutors have been heard to say, that the Quakers could not be overcome, and that the devil himself could not extirpate them."[10] Sewel begins his story with John Hus ("he sang with joy in the flames" [1:2]) and traces the lineage of the Quakers through the English separatist tradition, emphasizing the Elizabethan separatist martyrs Barrow, Greenwood, and Penry. The drama that he unfolds, chiefly by following the careers of the principal Quaker leaders, displays the extremes of good and evil characteristic of the tradition of Christian martyrology. Violent persecutors given to "cruel whippings, cutting off of ears, smotherings in prisons" are arrayed against virtuous Quakers who endure persecution with "extraordinary meekness, sincere love, ardent zeal, undaunted courage, and unshaken steadfastness" (1:11). Sewel's lively narrative, often supplemented by documents such as letters or petitions, gives a more complex and revealing picture of Quaker experience than his moralizing comments would suggest. Yet the movement he portrays has become orderly and decorous. Like Penn, Sewel sought to counter any sense of the Quakers as an unruly and destabilizing force. He describes the

Quakers as having earned the liberty of public worship they enjoyed under Queen Anne through "long suffering patience, a peaceable deportment, and a dutiful fidelity to the government set over them" (2:676).[11]

Besse's task differed from Sewel's, and Penn's, in that he was charged with collecting and publicizing the whole range of Quaker "sufferings," from seizures of property to prison deaths, but he presented these as part of the larger story of progress through suffering whose outlines were clearly defined by the time he wrote. In his preface Besse quotes two biblical passages that undergird much protestant understanding of suffering and that must have seemed particularly applicable to the Quaker experience, 2 Tim. 3:12 ("All that live godly in Christ Jesus, shall suffer Persecution") and Exod. 1:12 ("The more they afflicted them, the more they multiplied and grew"). For Quakers, living godly in Christ came to mean testifying forthrightly for their beliefs, as Besse shows that George Fox did when he went into a place of worship "and there declared the Testimony of Truth to the Priest and People" (1:552) and as numerous Quakers did when they offered particular "testimonies" by refusing to swear oaths, to remove their hats, to use familiar forms of address, or to pay tithes or church rates. He portrays them as called by God to declare their faith in these ways, driven by the felt necessity of "publishing the Truth."

Besse characterizes the posture with which Quakers responded to the persecution that such acts inevitably aroused in familiar ways, emphasizing their patience and constancy and, frequently, their joyful acceptance of suffering. He suggests the deliberate, moral character of these acts by attributing them to conscience ("the Testimony of a *good Conscience*, bearing Witness to the Truth" [1:1]) and tends to elide differences among Quakers in an idealizing vision of unity in the Spirit. One of his professed purposes was to show the support of communal worship in encouraging Quakers "cheerfully to undergo not only spoiling of their Goods, but Imprisonments, Banishments, and even Death itself, for they stood fast in one Spirit with one Mind, striving together for the Truth of the Gospel, and in nothing terrified of their Adversaries" (1:lii). Besse characterizes his own act of writing as his "testimony" to the memory of those who suffered and professes the hope that they will prove exemplary to his own slacker age. When George Fox first instructed Quakers to record and publicize their sufferings, he saw this as a means of exposing the nature of the persecution and influencing judges and others responsible for it.[12] At Besse's remove, such sufferings function primarily as reminders of the strenuous faith of those who participated in the heroic beginnings of the movement.

In reading Besse's *Sufferings* one is struck by the massive repetition, as Besse describes hundreds of similar acts in his county by county survey. Many of the accounts are brief, and he often simply lists those whose property was seized by distraint to discharge fines (typically for failure to attend the parish church or to pay tithes), sometimes with parallel columns demonstrating how much the value of the goods seized exceeded the fines. The cumulative detail, along with the more arresting accounts of beatings and prison abuses, has the effect of exposing the persecution in all its variations and of dramatizing the breadth and intensity of the Quaker resistance. Besse's attempt at inclusiveness also has a democratizing effect, since we read not only of Quaker leaders, some like William Penn and Isaac Penington from privileged social classes, but also of a seemingly inexhaustible company of merchants, artisans, laborers, and poor widows prepared to offer their testimonies. The act of naming was significant in itself, particularly in a publication commissioned by the Society of Friends (through the agency of the London Meeting for Sufferings) and intended to make available to a wider audience the body of recorded sufferings. Besse reinforced the importance of naming by providing indices of the names of sufferers by counties and another of those who "died under sufferings for their Religious Testimony" (2:634), the great majority of these victims of mistreatment or unsanitary conditions in prisons. His two large volumes function in part as a memorial, faithfully recording the names of those who suffered as we might those of war dead on a public monument, by this act not only honoring the individuals but giving their particular testimonies a continuing life.

As I have suggested, the themes of Besse's story of Quaker sufferings conform to the tradition of Christian martyrology, particularly as this had been shaped by John Foxe. He characterizes persecutors as raging, with a "furious and ignorant zeal" (1:501), and shows them suffering judgments of God, if not with the frequency they do in the *Acts and Monuments* or in early Quaker writing.[13] He represents the victims of persecution as alike in their ability to endure suffering in the cause of truth. Yet this drama took on a distinctive shape for Quakers and other nonconformists in late seventeenth-century England. The persecutors have become justices of the peace, sheriffs, mayors, and unsympathetic judges seen as applying the penal laws relentlessly, along with venal informers and abusive jailors. Persecution itself assumed new forms in the widespread use of distraints and the penalty of *praemunire*, entailing loss of property rights, to bring economic hardship or ruin. The Quaker Act added the penalty of banishment, after a third conviction, but this was imposed relatively infrequently and not always carried out.[14] The greatest hazard faced by most Quakers was imprisonment, with potential loss of livelihood and significant risk of disease and death.

Much of the violence Besse recounts takes the form of assaults on property. His accounts of "distresses" track the seizing of livestock, crops, and household goods, even bread from the oven, in painstaking detail. Such seizures could take violent and arbitrary forms, as when informers ("Devourers") break into a merchant's shop without a warrant, take what they please, and sell it with no reckoning given. Or when the sheriff's officers take possession of a house for days, terrorizing the occupants by "swearing and hectoring in a most insolent manner" (1:514). With an instinct for pathos that recalls Foxe, Besse dramatizes numerous abuses of the poor and vulnerable, such as the widows in Cheshire who were "bereft of all their Goods, till they had not a Skillet left to boil their childrens food in" (1:105). He describes a blind woman of eighty losing all her household goods including her bed for not attending the parish church. Such incidents illustrate what prisoners in Norwich, in a letter quoted by Besse, describe as the "Havock that has been made upon our Goods . . . by Bayliffs and mercenary Informers who have not only abused us, but have domineered over and abused the Justices and Justice itself" (1:515). Besse represents this "Havock" as involving acts of striking inhumanity and reducing many Quakers to economic ruin or near ruin. Given the fact that Quakers refused to pay even the most modest fines for reasons of religious principle, such economic persecution could be devastating.

Besse shows another kind of havoc visited upon the bodies of Quakers, initially for acts such as interrupting ministers in their churches or preaching in the streets and subsequently for continuing to meet despite the increasingly severe prohibitions of the various Acts intended to suppress dissent. The "wicked rabble" is an active player in Besse's drama of persecution, materializing to shout verbal abuse, throw dirt, and strike blows.[15] The physical violence that Besse reports, often quoting contemporary accounts, frequently appears as a kind of mindless fury, an upwelling of bigotry and hatred triggered by the unconventional behavior of Quakers and frequently encouraged by "priests" or local officials. Quaker bashing could take many forms. The "rabble" of Besse's accounts may be occupants of a village gathering to drive away itinerant Quakers perceived as challenging the local religious order or Cambridge students rampaging noisily through a meeting and assaulting the speaker, who persists "undismayed," as senior fellows of their college look on (1:86–7). In the 1660s and 1670s attacks of soldiers on Quaker meetings represent a more deliberate kind of campaign based in part on perceptions of the Quaker movement as a dangerous political force. In his record of sufferings in London Besse describes repeated instances in which soldiers break into established meeting places, such as the Bull and Mouth, beat the participants, and carry large numbers of them off to Newgate. Besse shows Quakers as suffering such violence without resisting and as continuing to meet, in the street when unable to meet elsewhere. He reports that seventy Quakers pulled out of a meeting at Westminster were "beaten, bruised, and had their clothes torn by Soldiers and others, dragged by the Hair of the Head, and some of them knockt down" (1:366). Soldiers break up a meeting in Grace-church Street by drumming to drown out the speakers, a favorite tactic, driving a coach and horses through the crowd, and finally using their muskets as clubs: "[they] pusht down both men and Women with their muskets, and tore Mary Wicks's Scarf and Apron, and pincht her" (1:413). Such particularity, to the point of specifying the exact nature of the offense to Mary Wicks, was a way of dramatizing the confrontation between force and unresisting weakness and the indignities Quakers exposed themselves to by continuing to meet.

Imprisonment constituted the most severe trial for Quakers, and Besse gave accounts of prison experience the kind of prominence that Foxe gave to the burnings of martyrs. Cragg has described the prison conditions that made imprisonment an ordeal for nonconformists: crowding, filth, foul air, extremes of heat and cold, abuse by jailers.[16] The phrase "stinking prison" becomes almost formulaic in the accounts of prison life that Besse quotes or summarizes. He dramatizes extreme conditions, such as the crowding caused by committing so many to Newgate after arrests for unlawful meetings that they had no room to sit or lie down, as well as individual acts of cruelty. Besse shows Sir Richard Brown, the Lord Mayor of London in the early 1660s who pursued Quakers with particular zeal, dismissing a Quaker's request to visit his wife in prison, "Let her die there and rot, thee mayst get another Wife the sooner" (1:367), and then sending the husband to Newgate for asking. Foxe had demonized persecutors, as Eusebius had in his *Ecclesiastical History* (the Roman consuls and emperors who rage against the early Christians). Besse singles out particularly relentless or callous enemies of Quakers who had achieved notoriety, giving evil an array of human faces.

The more hostile the local officials or judges and the more abusive the jailers, the more extraordinary the capacity of Quakers to endure suffering patiently would seem. As Besse makes clear through his comments and those he reports, the model for such acceptance of suffering was Christ. Thomas Speed tells the Mayor of Bristol, in a letter Besse includes, that he is persecuting Jesus "in his suffering members" (1:46). In embracing suffering, and professing to forgive their enemies, Quakers that Besse quotes identify with Christ, confident that they will be strengthened by God to endure their trials. In their letters and petitions prisoners credit divine comfort for their ability to endure the unspeakable conditions that they itemize: "But in this is our Rejoicing, that they cannot keep God from us, by whose Power we are kept in Patience to suffer these Things" (1:73). Besse represents the constancy of those who die in prison as dependent upon grace. After naming seven who died in Northamptonshire in 1664, he asserts that the Lord "had armed them with the Patience of Saints to undergo Tribulations and afflictions for Testimony he had called them to bear" (1:519). They were even able to sing praises to God, Besse reports, "to the Astonishment of others who beheld their Piety and Patience."

Spectacular cases, such as that of James Parnell of Essex, offered a particularly dramatic way of reinforcing the ideal of patient suffering. Parnell died at nineteen in Colchester Castle after being beaten by the jailer's wife and her servant, denied food, being forced to sleep on the stone floor, and finally confined to a damp hole in the castle wall that could only be reached by a ladder and a rope. Besse describes his constitution as ruined by further "cruel Usage" and serious injuries resulting from a fall from the ladder onto the stones below. He portrays Parnell as saintly throughout his ordeal, displaying "remarkable Innocence, Patience, and Magnanimity" (1:92). Sewel had given a fuller and more detailed account of the case, on which Besse appears to have drawn,[17] including scenes from the period before the imprisonment. In one of these a townsperson strikes Parnell with a "great staff," shouting "There, take that for Christ's sake," to which Parnell responds, "Friend, I do receive it for Jesus Christ's sake" (196).[18] Sewel concludes his account of Parnell's experience by pronouncing "Thus this valiant soldier of the Lamb conquered through sufferings" (201). He drew out the dramatic potential of Parnell's story more fully than did Besse, constrained by the need to give an accounting of all the reported suffering in Essex and perhaps lacking Sewel's narrative skills.

The story of James Parnell suggests one way Besse's work avoids simply becoming a register of names and incidents. While the structure and purposes of his *Sufferings* precluded the kind of continuous narrative Sewel offers, Besse provides his readers with numerous mini-dramas. These can involve the prison deaths of Quaker leaders, trials or examinations that Besse reports at length (records of these were a particularly rich source), or particular persecutions and the suffering they occasioned. Besse frequently uses small dramas involving more obscure Quakers to show how God intervenes to punish or frustrate their enemies. He tells the story of Oliver Atherton dying in a Lancashire prison in 1663 for not paying tithes, at the suit of the Countess of Derby, who refuses an appeal from his son and proves "inexorable" against others as well. Three weeks after Atherton's body is carried through Ormkirk to burial, the Countess's own body makes the same journey (1:311). Like those who reported the event, Besse read it as a judgment of God, in this case all the more significant because of the dramatic way it collapsed differences of social class.

Besse's account of the sufferings in Bristol, the second port after London and an important center of Quaker activity, offers a good example of the way patterns and individual dramas can emerge from what may seem at times to be a relatively shapeless chronicle. In this account, as in others, Besse records the ebb and flow of hostilities against the Quakers, describing "storm(s) of persecution" and periods of relative peace.[19] Some of these storms are triggered by particular individuals, some by external events such as the uprising of Fifth Monarchy men led by Thomas Venner in January of 1661, which sharply increased suspicion of all radical dissenters, or the passing of the Second Conventicle Act in 1670. Besse also registers changing patterns of persecution. His traverses of the 1650s include frequent accounts of beatings of individuals who can be identified as Quakers and of arrests of itinerant preachers for vagrancy. Besse shows Edward Burrough and Frances Howgill arrested in Bristol for drawing crowds on one occasion (the warrant calls them Franciscans "under the Notion of *Quakers*" [1:40]). In another incident typical of the early days of the movement Besse describes the imprisonment of Sarah Goldsmith for standing at the gates of Bristol in sackcloth and ashes as a sign against pride. Interestingly, we hear nothing of the most flamboyant and controversial act of this period, James Nayler's ride into Bristol on an ass in October of 1656 in apparent imitation of Christ, or of his being whipped through the streets of Bristol as part of the severe punishment for blasphemy imposed upon him by Parliament. The behavior of Nayler and the followers who hailed him as the Son of God no doubt seemed such an egregious example of the excesses of the early Quakers to Besse that he did not want to remind his readers of the details. He does describe a penitent Nayler and print his "Recantation" in his account of sufferings in London.[20] His accounts of subsequent decades in Bristol focus on the arrests of established groups of Quakers who persist in meeting despite the penal acts and on their subsequent efforts to dramatize prison conditions and seek relief through petitions and letters.

Besse gives the most attention to two notable periods of persecution in Bristol, focussing on some exceptional villains and the heroism of local Quakers in enduring their abuses.[21] He presents Sir John Knight the elder, mayor in 1663–64, as obsessed by his enmity toward Quakers, although in fact he pursued other nonconformists as well. Knight as mayor sends the militia to break up Quaker meetings and tries to manipulate the legal system, in part by choleric outbursts in court, to make sure that the Quaker leaders end up in prison. Besse reports that as a member of the House of

Commons Knight worked for the Conventicle Act (1664) and "wept for Joy at the passing of it" (1:51), then shows him vigorously pursuing Quakers in an effort to convict as many as possible three times before his term of office expires so that they will be subject to the new penalty of banishment. He makes Knight appear more monstrous by showing the sailors asked to transport banished Quakers refusing and by describing the citizens of Bristol as alienated by Knight's "violent proceedings" and allowing Quaker meetings to resume after his mayoralty.

Another Sir John Knight, cousin of the first and sheriff in the early 1680s, surfaces at the center of an even more furious storm of persecution that began in 1681 acting in concert with the notorious persecutor John Hellier, a lawyer.[22] Besse comments after describing Knight and Hellier breaking up one meeting and sending ninety Quakers to Bridewell, "And so they were driven away *like sheep to the Slaughter* (1:63)," invoking a biblical phrase (Rom. 8:36, Ps. 44:22) regularly used of protestant martyrs. Besse's sense of the vulnerability of the Quakers and the callousness of persecutors emerges perhaps most clearly in a motif that he develops here and throughout his *Sufferings*, that of violence toward women. He shows Hellier and others urged on by him calling Quaker women whores and tearing their hoods and scarves. Hearing Dorcas Dole at prayer in Bridewell, Hellier causes her to be pulled off her knees "by Violence" and confined in a close, dark place in which she faints (1:66). Besse describes the children of the Quakers as continuing to meet during this period in the absence of the imprisoned adults, "with a remarkable Gravity and Composure," despite the fact that Hellier would appear in his "Fury" to beat them with a "twisted Whalebone stick" (1:66). He renders the spirit of persecution, embodied here by Hellier, as one of uncontrolled rage against those who persist in their nonconformist behavior.

The experience of the Quaker prisoners, presented largely through their own words, dominates the last part of Besse's account of Bristol. He includes a cautionary tale about Isaac Dennis, the notorious keeper of Newgate, who appears as the archetypal abusive jailer of nonconformist literature. Besse used extracts from a contemporary account to show Dennis's brutality toward prisoners: beating them, throwing them down stairs, locking them in nasty rooms, breaking up meetings for worship in prison. The heart of the drama, however, lay in Dennis's sudden reversal after being visited with "judgments" from God that leave him in agony and unable to eat or sleep. He asks and receives forgiveness from the prisoners but is unable to experience true repentance and dies in misery, "a Warning to all" (1:71). One is prepared for Knight and Hellier to be struck down by similar judgments, but instead Knight becomes Sir John while the prisoners document their mistreatment over a period of years without receiving any relief, despite appeals on their behalf by sympathetic citizens alienated by Knight's cruelty and abuses of his authority.

Besse brings his account of Bristol to a close with two letters from the prisoners to the yearly meeting at London that profess their good spirits and acceptance of their suffering and demonstrate a sense of community intensified by the experience of persecution which recalls that revealed in the letters of Foxe's Marian martyrs. Printing such letters, and other documents such as petitions from those offering to take the places of prisoners suffering particular hardships, was a way for Besse to demonstrate what he saw as the unity and loving spirit of the besieged Quakers and to affirm the ideal of patient suffering. In the case of Bristol, Besse could achieve a satisfying sense of closure by celebrating the proclamation of James II in 1685 pardoning the prisoners: "Thus it pleased God in his merciful Providence to work Deliverance for his People in a singular and extraordinary manner, by making even a *Popish* King instrumental in his Hand for opening the Prison Doors" (1:74). He does not always draw out such a sense of providential design, commonly ending his accounts by simply reporting the last instance of suffering in a particular county.

The ongoing drama that Besse presents in his *Sufferings* is one in which we see institutional power and violence of many kinds arrayed against weakness; it was natural for him to imagine persecutors as "Wolves" harrying "the poor sheep of Christ" (1:170). Besse offers moralizing commentary on the "outragious Violence" directed against Quakers and, repeatedly, on the Christlike patience of the persecuted. His comment on a letter from prisoners in Ilchester to their "Companions in Tribulation" in London's Newgate prison is typical: "This letter savours of the Humility, Patience, and Resignation of faithful Sufferers" (1:590). Yet, as we have seen, the weak also have their victories. Providential acts can bring a reversal of fortunes, as when James II's pardon releases the prisoners of Bristol or when, after a series of delays, Quakers being transported to Jamaica are captured by Dutch privateers and returned to England (1:406). Enemies of the Quakers are stricken by judgments of God; sympathetic citizens or officials may thwart the designs of persecutors. And, as Besse delights in showing, Quakers may defeat their assailants by their very willingness to suffer. He portrays troopers in Essex who beat Quakers with clubs studded with iron spikes relenting upon "finding the constancy of the Sufferers invincible" and becoming ashamed of fighting those "whom no Abuses could provoke to resist them" (1:200). Solomon Eccles literally turns the other cheek, more than once, to absorb blows from the secretary of the Bishop of Gloucester, thereby "obtaining a *Christian Conquest* over his Opposer" (1:216).

Such victories are consistent with Besse's portrayal of Quakers as victims, "poor sheep of Christ," yet there is another strain in his *Sufferings* and in much Quaker writing that reveals a more aggressive stance and that can be characterized, in New Testament terms, as boldness in the name of God. Peter and John display such boldness before the Sadducees, and the apostles and Paul are described as speaking "boldly" in declaring the message of the Gospel.[23] The Quaker commitment to bold speaking is perhaps most apparent in their habit of challenging ministers in their own pulpits, including those of other dissenting sects, but one sees it as well in their conduct in examinations and trials. Besse reports with apparent approval the resistance of itinerant Quakers to interrogations aimed at demonstrating that they were dangerous vagrants. He shows John Audland and John Wilkinson, apprehended at a meeting they are leading, responding to the magistrates' question, "What Business have you here?" with "We came to bear Witness to the Truth" (1:43), rejecting the terms of the discourse in the fashion of other early Quakers who responded to examiners' questions about where they came from by insisting that they lived in the land of Canaan. Besse's accounts of trials illustrate the persistence and increasing skill of Quakers in contesting the legal tactics as well as the assumptions of the justices. He presents the famous trial of William Penn and William Meade at the Old Bailey in 1670 as a contest between the arbitrary power of magistrates and the "just and ancient Liberties of the People of England" invoked by Penn (1:416). Penn demonstrates a kind of boldness in the cause of truth that Besse and other Quaker apologists valued, challenging the indictment and accusing the judge of making the jury a "nose of wax" (by sending it back three times in an unsuccessful attempt to get the verdict he wanted).[24] Penn, and Besse, saw no incompatibility between this kind of bold speaking, warranted by the example of the apostles, and acceptance of suffering. Penn's parting remarks on another occasion, when he was sentenced to six months in Newgate for speaking at an unlawful meeting, illustrate the way a Christlike posture could become a vehicle for defying one's enemies and declaring a spiritual victory: "I scorn that Religion that is not worth Suffering for, and able to sustain them that are afflicted for it. . . . Thy Religion persecutes, and mine forgives: and I desire my God to forgive you all that are concerned with my commitment, and I leave you all in perfect Charity, wishing your everlasting salvation"(1:435).

One sees another form of bold speaking in letters and petitions seeking relief from persecution and oppressive prison conditions. These might begin with the writers portraying themselves as "the poor oppressed and Suffering People of God" (1:520), then go on to offer a passionate indictment of the injustice of magistrates and the abuses of jailers. Besse praises the bluntness of such accusations as "Plainness of Stile" in describing a letter from George Fox to the magistrates who imprisoned him in Derbyshire (1:137). He describes a letter from prisoners in Yorkshire to the king as displaying "innocent Boldness" and "Christian Plainness" in its candor and avoidance of conventional flattery (2:160). Besse clearly did not regard such bold speaking as incompatible with his story of Quakers as prevailing through their capacity for patient suffering, but there are times when the boldness of the words he reports seem at odds with his own tendency to praise patience and humility. He risks undermining his efforts to portray a stabler and more decorous Quakerism, unlikely to pose a threat to existing institutions, by giving space to much more strident voices than his own.

One occasionally hears in Besse's *Sufferings* the prophetic vehemence so characteristic of early Quaker tracts in prisoners' letters warning of the "Wrath of the Lamb" (1:87) or the impending "Day of Vengeance upon the Wicked" (1:384). George Whitehead, eulogizing Edward Burrough for his patience after his death in Newgate, describes him as caught up in glory beyond the reach of his persecutors, "who shall be broken and laid low in the desolation and ruin of *Babylon*" (1:391). Such linguistic violence clashes with Besse's voice and with those of other Quakers he quotes, such as Frances Howgill on his deathbed, proclaiming the sweetness of suffering. The inherent tension between the posture of patient suffering and the aggressiveness of bold speaking and bold acting was endemic to Quakerism and to other protestant movements defined by resistance to persecution. It is a prominent feature of John Foxe's accounts of the Marian martyrs and of the tradition of protestant martyrology he inaugurated. The fact that relatively little of the threatening language of the early Quakers found its way into Besse's *Sufferings*, however, suggests that he was more comfortable representing a suffering people than a sometimes fiercely oppositional one. To speak of "innocent" boldness and "Christian" plainness was to make aggressiveness seem more palatable. Besse contracted the distance between the extremes of Quaker behavior that one finds in Fox's *Journal*, itself toned down by Thomas Ellwood's editing but still showing Fox moving between Christlike acceptance of beatings and prison hardships, on the one hand, and prophetic denunciations and exultant proclamations of victory over his enemies on the other. The basic story Besse had to tell was the one he summarized in his conclusion, that of how a religious people, "for the Exercise of a good Conscience," endured "a violent Storm of Persecution of near forty Years Continuance" that "rendered the Constancy, Faith, and Patience of the Sufferers the more approved and conspicuous" (2:534) and ensured the growth and survival of their movement. His condensation of the vast literature of sufferings provided eighteenth-century Quakers with a vivid sense of the heroic exploits of their predecessors and at the same time reassured them that the storms of persecution and the extreme responses to the leadings of the Holy Spirit that sometimes accompanied them were safely in the past.

NOTES

1. Craig Horle, *The Quakers and the English Legal System, 1660–1688* (Philadelphia University of Pennsylvania Press, 1988), preface. Richard Greaves has shown the unevenness of the persecution of nonconformists generally, citing cases in which local officials refused to prosecute or imposed light penalties. See *Enemies Under His Feet* (Stanford: Stanford University Press, 1990), 132–42 and *passim*.

2. I am thinking particularly of the work of Barry Reay and Christopher Hill. See Reay's *The Quakers and the English Revolution* (London: Temple Smith, 1985) and Hill's *The World Turned Upside Down* (London: Temple Smith, 1972) and *The Experience of Defeat* (London: Faber, 1984). The earlier work of Hugh Barbour, *The Quakers in Puritan England* (New Haven: Yale University Press, 1964), and Richard Vann, *The Social Development of English Quakerism, 1655-1755* (Cambridge, Mass.: Cambridge University Press, 1969), remains indispensable. For an extended narrative charting the development of Quakerism in seventeenth-century England, see William C. Braithwaite's *The Beginnings of Quakerism*, 2d ed. (Cambridge: Cambridge University Press, 1955) and *The Second Period of Quakerism*, 2d ed. (Cambridge: Cambridge University Press, 1961).

3. Besse's project originated in a mandate from the London Meeting for Sufferings in 1727 to put the accumulated records of sufferings in order. A plan to abridge these for publication as an *Abstract* of sufferings for the period 1650–60 was abandoned after three volumes. The form of the eventual *Sufferings* resulted from a series of interactions between Besse and the Meeting for Sufferings. For an account of this history and an examination of Besse's use of sources, see Richard Vann's "Friends Sufferings – Collected and Recollected," *Quaker History* 61 (1972), 24–35. An unattributed article, "The Story of a Great Literary Venture," *Journal of the Friends' Historical Society* 23 (1926), 1–11, details Besse's financial dealings with the Meeting for Sufferings.

4. In *Discourses of Martyrdom in English Literature, 1563–1694* (Cambridge: Cambridge University Press, 1993), 218–23. In the book I discuss the relationship of Besse's *Sufferings* to Foxe's *Acts and Monuments* and Besse's uses of the language of martyrdom, particularly to develop the theme of the sweetness of suffering.

5. Vann compared Besse's work with records of sufferings for Buckinghamshire, Norwich, and Norfolk and in manuscripts preserved in London and found that he omitted some incidents and also included others not found in the relevant volumes of the Meeting for Sufferings. He notes that "given the attitudes of Friends and the state of historical scholarship in his times" it is hard to imagine that Besse could have been "any more accurate or complete." See Vann, "Friends Sufferings," 32–4. Horle finds Besse a useful source but observes that he omits valuable details and gives the impression of "unduly harsh and continuous enforcement." Horle, *The Quakers and the English Legal System*, xiiin.

6. Besse, *A Collection of the Sufferings of the People called Quakers, for the Testimony of a Good Conscience*, 2 vols. (London, 1753), 1:2. Further references will be given in the text.

7. *Select Works of William Penn* (London, 1771), 770.

8. This was first articulated and publicized by Fox and other leaders in a Declaration in January of 1661.

9. This was first published in Low Dutch in Amsterdam in 1717 and subsequently translated and adapted by Sewel, who was the grandson of a Brownist who had emigrated to Holland. For information on Sewel and the evolution and reception of his *History*, see William I. Hull, *William Sewel of Amsterdam, 1653-1720* (Philadelphia: Swarthmore College Monographs on Quaker History, 1933).

10. William Sewel, *The History of the People Called Quakers*, 2 vols. (London, 1795), 2:430. Further references will be given in the text.

11. Sewel's work illustrates the growing tendency to omit the excesses of the early Quakers. He notes that he did not feel bound to notice every "odd case" (1:xi). He describes his parents, interestingly, as the first "orthodox" Quakers in Amsterdam, distinguishing them from questionable types drawn to the movement.

12. See George Fox, *A Collection of Many Select and Christian Epistles*, 2 vols. (Philadelphia and New York, 1831), 1: 134–6 (epistles CXL and CXLI, 1657). Fox also grasped the potential of publishing excesses of persecutors for engendering popular support, as H. Larry Ingle has shown in his recent biography. Ingle describes Fox as remaining in Launceston jail beyond the point at which he could have left in order to continue to portray himself as a martyr in a stream of leaflets and broadsides. *First Among Friends: George Fox and the Creation of Quakerism* (Oxford: Oxford University Press, 1994), 139–40.

13. Vann discusses some instances in which Besse omitted or toned down accounts of judgments. See "Friends Sufferings," 34–5. Besse nonetheless includes some lurid cases, such as that of the Dorsetshire man who wrapped himself in a bull's hide and injured a Quaker preacher's lip with a horn and was then gored through the chin at a bull-baiting shortly thereafter, dying instantly, "a singular instance of divine justice" (1:166).

14. See Gerald R. Cragg, *Puritanism in the Period of the Great Persecution, 1660–1688* (Cambridge: Cambridge University Press, 1957), 55. Four Quakers were condemned and hanged in Boston, and widely celebrated as martyrs, but this practice was quickly stopped by Charles II. See *Sufferings*, 2:204ff.

15. Cf. George Fox's accounts of the "rude people" throwing dirt and stones, beating, and otherwise physically abusing Quakers. John L. Nickalls, ed., *The Journal of George Fox* (Cambridge: Cambridge University Press, 1952), pp.127–8, 276, 308, 310, 352, 403, and *passim*.

16. Cragg, *Puritanism in the Period of the Great Persecution*, chap. 4. Cf. George Fox's graphic accounts of the prison conditions he experienced, for example, in the notorious Doomsdale: "what with the stink and what with the smoke, we were like to be choked and smothered. . . . we could not sit down the place being so full of prisoners' excrements." *Journal*, 253.

17. Sewel reports conversations with eyewitnesses and claims to have crawled into the hole in which Parnell was confined to see what it was like. Besse follows Sewel closely, sometimes echoing his phrasing.

18. This anecdote appears in Stephen Crisp's testimony concerning Parnell, reprinted in Hugh Barbour and Arthur O. Roberts, *Early Quaker Writings, 1650–1700* (Grand Rapids: Eerdmans, 1973), pp.164–6. Crisp was a likely source for Sewel, as was Ellis Hookes, who describes Parnell's prison ordeal in detail in another of the testimonies that preface the posthumous edition of Parnell's work, *A collection of the several writings* (London, 1675).

19. I do not find that Besse makes persecution seem so continuous as Horle does, although his exclusive focus on sufferings may give this impression.

20. In his recantation Nayler denounces the "ranting wild Spirits" that gathered about him in his "Time of Darkness" and urges wariness of "Voices, Visions, and Revelations." Besse characterizes Nayler as enduring his punishment "with a Patience astonishing to his Beholders" and as restored by God to a "true Sense of Religion" (1:362–5). Sewel (256–66) tells the story of Nayler's ride and his subsequent punishment in detail, declaring that his "sorrowful fall ought to stand as a warning" (256) to others to continue in humility.

21. Edward Terrill's contemporary *Records* of the Broadmead Chapel of Bristol distinguish ten separate persecutions and give by far the fullest account of the persecution of Bristol nonconformists in the period. See Roger Hayden, ed., *The Records of a Church of Christ in Bristol* ([Bristol]: Bristol Record Society, 1974), which includes a substantial introduction by Hayden. The experience of persecution recorded by Terrill resembles that described by Besse

(and Sewel) in many respects but also reveals important differences in attitude, chiefly in the absence of the focus on suffering that characterizes Quaker writing. The Broadmead congregation attempted to keep their meeting house from being wrecked by paying a fine at one point and, with other nonconformist congregations, sought to avoid persecution in the 1680s by meeting in private houses and in the woods. Terrill notes that only the Quakers continued to meet in the vicinity of their meeting house, by then nailed shut (235).

22. Hellier appears as the most active and merciless enemy of nonconformists in Terrill's *Records*. Sewel calls him "brutish Helliar" and describes his "diabolical rage" against Quakers (424–5).

23. See, for example, Acts 4:13, 31; Eph. 6:20; Phil. 1:14, 20.

24. The trial is famous for having established the independence of the jury. See Cragg, *Puritanism in the Period of the Great Persecution*, 49–50.

Early Quakerism: A Historian's Afterword

ANN HUGHES

For historians, as for many literary scholars, the inspiration of Christopher Hill has been crucial to the study of radical politics and radical writing.[1] Hill's vivid evocation of the "world turned upside down" in the mid-seventeenth century has always been based on a close attention to the language and imagery of radical prose. Equally, Hill's influence is important to the widely accepted picture of the Quakers as a radical, activist grouping in the 1650s, in contrast to the respectable, authoritarian, pacifist movement dominated by Fox after the Restoration.[2] Recently, however, historical interests in printed literature and in radical religion have become more diffuse or more apologetic. In Hill's writing, the radical and the popular are often seen as identical, while the most recent general account of the Quakers during the English revolution, by a scholar working consciously in the Hill tradition, announced itself as, amongst other things, "an essay in popular history."[3] This identification has become more difficult to sustain in the light of revisionist histories of the Reformation which have stressed the exclusionary and inaccessible aspects of Protestantism rather than its emancipatory potential.[4] Working within this framework John Morrill has insisted on the strength of traditional, conservative or Anglican responses to the religious upheavals of the 1650s; if any religious impulse was "popular" it was this, rather than Puritan reform or radical separatism.[5] Consequently, a collection of essays on radical religion in the English Revolution included a rather defensive preface which denied any "intention to minimize the importance of popular conservatism in English religious history."[6]

There has thus been something of a loss of confidence amongst historians in the importance of radicalism in the English revolution, and more work has probably been done in literary studies than in history over the last decade. The broad historical surveys of radicalism in the 1980s paid little attention to the literary aspects of Quaker tracts; there was little concern for intended audiences, publishing strategies, stylistic devices and so on. Rather tracts were used for their content only, for a guide to the programmes and beliefs of radical groups. Indeed there was more interest in the geographical "spread" of Quakerism or in the social characteristics of its adherents than in the movement's use of print culture.[7] A striking attempt to consider some of these issues has come, as it were, from another direction in Colin Davis's controversial discussion of the Ranters.

Davis made some interesting suggestions about the publishing and rhetorical strategies of the alarmed conservatives and heresiographers who, he claims, constructed a "Ranter myth." Paradoxically, though, he gives less attention to the possible intentions of radical writers themselves. Why and how did Bauthumley, Coppe and Clarkson turn to print as a means of communication? What audience did they envisage for their works? What is the significance of the stylistic devices they adopted?[8] Such investigations may be as important as the search to define or eliminate a shared content in their writings.

While many historians of early modern England, as of other fields, have become more concerned with issues of culture and language in recent years, they have tended to focus on the period before 1640, rather than on the years of civil war and revolution.[9] Much of this work has significant implications for the radical politics and religion of the 1640s and 1650s. Tessa Watt has examined the complex accommodations between zealous Protestantism, popular religious ideas and print culture, arguing that most cheap print – broadsheet ballads, woodcuts and "small books" – was traditional rather than reformed in tone. This might suggest that radical forms of Protestantism would not find broad favor after 1640, although we cannot be sure that those suspicious of the zealous Puritanism of the early seventeenth century would be even more hostile to interregnum radicalism. Nuanced, locally based studies of religious dissent may add more precision and complexity to our understanding of the "social appeal" of particular religious affiliations. But Watt has certainly illuminated a world where print was an ever-present part of daily life, not confined to the prosperous and the educated, but found decorating the homes and alehouses of comparatively humble people, and intimately intertwined with the oral world of poetry and song. By the 1620s there was an expanding market for religious literature when rising literacy rates and falling book prices made possible the invention of a new genre, the godly chapbook, available to husbandmen's and yeomen's households on a regular basis.[10] The manifold interconnections between oral culture, writing and commercial print culture are demonstrated also in the verse libels seventeenth-century villagers composed to ridicule their ministers, millers or landlords. Such rhymes might be echoes of already familiar printed ballads; equally some local oral compositions, suitably polished, might end up in print. In any village, it seems, the illiterate could find a friend or neighbor who could read or write down a verse or two for them; all were aware of the value of writing and print in spreading information and abuse. It is clear, furthermore, that more could read print than could decipher "written hand" – one of those obvious but forgotten points that can contribute to our understanding of the wide-ranging print culture of the 1640s and 1650s.[11]

If early seventeenth-century England was a society utterly familiar with writing and print; and if print was not something to be privately and passively consumed but inextricably connected with dynamic participation and activity, then historians may have become too pessimistic about the audience for, and impact of the radical printed prose of the revolutionary decades. When the Quakers attacked parish ministers by sending them provocative and insulting written queries, they were adopting a familiar form for novel, radical purposes.[12] The Quakers, as Kate Peters describes here, used printed tracts deliberately and self-consciously as aggressive propaganda and as a means of establishing the identity of an emergent movement, for both members and opponents. Here too, they were working with, not against the grain of contemporary culture, albeit with a dramatic intensity. The energetic use of print, coupled with a concern, from the start, for systematic record keeping was both cause and effect of the Quakers' success as a religious movement. From the start, Quakers tried to control both their contemporary identity and their historical reputation. This has meant that it remains impossible for historians to explain this radical movement away as a projection of conservative anxieties; there have also been problems, even for non-Quaker scholars, in seeing the Quakers in any other than their own terms. One of Reay's aims was to alleviate "what I perceive to be a major shortcoming in all studies of early Quakerism, the failure of its historians to make use of non-Quaker sources."[13] Using official, legal and anti-Quaker material, however, produced an argument that the main effect of the Quaker movement was to provoke a conservative reaction that formed a major motivation for the restoration of the monarchy.[14] A more positive understanding of Quaker agency, exploring the complex self-definition of the movement in the 1650s, and the means by which Quakers argued for their ideas in a hostile world, is crucial to historical reassessments of the importance of religious radicalism in the English revolution. Historians can build on the explorations of oral and print culture before the civil war; they can also gain immeasurably from the work of literary scholars. While historians were preoccupied with arid inconclusive debates about the social characteristics of Quakerism, literary scholars continued to study radical writing.[15] The articles in this volume suggest how historians might approach Quaker texts in a more sophisticated way, neither taking them on trust, nor dismissing them simply as biased propaganda. The insistence of Thomas Corns and John Knott, for example, on seeing crucial Quaker texts like Fox's Journal or Joseph Besse's *Collections of the Sufferings of the People Called Quakers* as literary productions, as works of artifice rather than as straightforward sources, is very important. Fox's text, written retrospectively but with manuscripts from the 1650s inserted, then further edited for publication, is usually seen as marking an important stage in the emergence of a more moderate and respectable Quaker movement, anxious to play down its radical past and to draw a veil over any possible challengers to Fox's authority (like Nayler). Corns's argument that the very complexity of the text prevented its serving such a purpose in an effective way forces some historical reappraisals. Knott's account of Besse as a "story" would seem to show why the assessment of a modern scholar of Quaker suffering is more nuanced than the Quakers' own accounts.[16] Conflicting contemporary accounts of Quaker martyrs offer further support to this argument. Knott, following Besse, writes of the young James Parnell being "denied food" in an Essex jail; the local Puritan minister Ralph Josselin described him in his diary as a deliberate self-starver: "heard this morning that James Parnel the father of the Quakers in these parts, having undertaken to fast 40 dayes and nights, was die 10 in the morning found dead."[17]

The seventeenth-century Quakers were both an ecstatic, mystical religious movement, and one that managed to have an ordered, instrumental attitude to self-presentation and the deployment of printed tracts. As Nigel Smith shows, these paradoxes allowed diversity and could lead to mis-recognitions between Quakers as well as a developed sense of identity. Further paradoxes emerge in the discussions of female Quaker activism and of gender relationships within the movement which have much occupied feminist historians and literary scholars. The diverse contributions of Burns, Gardiner and Hobby illustrate some of the debates, rehearsed also in the recent thorough and complex treatment of female prophecy and Quaker women by Phyllis Mack.[18] As Gardiner suggests, and Mack documents, the role of "Mother in Israel" legitimated female authority within the Quakers, but this was authority for some types of women in defined circumstances. It also endorsed the expression of female subjectivities, as Burns shows, but Mack argues that acceptable forms of female self-expression became more constraining, even masochistic, in the later seventeenth century. As Hobby stresses, the particular circumstances of the 1650s permitted a variety of political and apocalyptic writing by women which was less often sanctioned in the Restoration period. It remains unclear, however, how significant the differences were between male and female writing in the 1650s – how far maternal and other types of feminine imagery influenced the movement as a whole, rather than empowering women specifically. As always in discussions of women, there are diverse experiences, tensions and qualifications to be made but seventeenth-century Quaker women were remarkable by any standards. Elaine Hobby has shown that they dominated women's published writing in the 1650s, while Patricia

Crawford calculated that the published works of female Quakers made up as much as twenty per cent of all seventeenth-century women's publications.[19]

Gender is a central part of the story of the Quaker move from activism to quietist respectability. It is argued that the establishment of an approved, formal but carefully circumscribed role for women in the separate women's meetings of the 1670s marked a retreat from the audacity of the prophets and missionaries of the 1650s. There are ambiguities here however, for, as Mack stresses, the women's meetings gave some women (respectable "mothers in Israel") formal jurisdiction over aspects of male behaviour and the Quakers remain to this day a movement that women have found empowering. Historians are always skeptical of spectacular claims such as Mack's view that Quaker women's meetings were "a cradle not only of modern feminism but of the movements of abolitionism, women's suffrage and peace activism, all of which were, and are, enlivened by the presence (even predominance) of Quaker female leaders."[20] But there is more validity in this claim than in most.

The story of the transformation of the Quakers is widely accepted: the ecstatic, revolutionary movement of the 1650s, when as Loewenstein writes "the Quakers waged war against the world," turned into a sober, respectable, self-disciplined movement dominated by Fox, and by a complex bureaucratic organization. But we need to recognize that this is a story, a neat narrative that can be too much taken for granted. As already suggested, Corns's discussion of Fox's Journal highlights problems and contradictions in this process. It was not only that "powerful elements of enigma and bewilderment" inevitably accompanied attempts to convey in language what remained essentially uncommunicable and mysterious – the workings of God's spirit, and the impact of Fox's own proselytizing. The structure of the work, with its layers of revision and the insertion of documents from the 1650s made it a very uncertain way of creating a moderate polemic. One obvious example is in the way a more favorable picture of Oliver Cromwell than was politic kept breaking through.[21] Contradictions are revealed even in the gentlemanly William Penn writing "with the ease of a man of the world" – but also in an "incantatory, repetitive manner"; and also often clearly luxuriating in what he denounced.[22]

As Peters shows, the Quakers were remarkable constructors and keepers of their own traditions; they were meticulous record keepers, preserving correspondence, records of sufferings, autobiographies and missionary material as well as maintaining control of their printed material. I have already suggested how this has affected historical interpretations of the Quakers, which have often been closely based on Fox and Besse. However this very involvement in their own past meant that the drive to moderate respectability was always liable to be not quite sabotaged but qualified by this living, more radical tradition. Here this is demonstrated in Corns's article; in Smith's account of the survival of Naylerite practices after 1660; and in Knott's account of Besse where the "linguistic violence" of the original petitions, prison letters, and trial narratives quoted undermined the compiler's aim of decorum and control. Although Besse was "more comfortable representing a suffering people than a sometimes fiercely oppositional one," his own sources cut across this.

The Quakers' subsequent development cannot of course be connected simply to the ways they recorded their own history. The Muggletonians, also, were "great hoarders," but that sect's refusal to evangelize, waiting instead for "lost sheep" to seek them out, gravely limited their impact after the Restoration.[23] Nonetheless the Quakers' concern to keep their past alive, to record it so carefully, contributed to the perennial tensions within the movement between diversity and discipline, respectability and mystical communion with God. The radical writing of the 1650s could not be forgotten and helped legitimate later Quaker activism and criticism of the established order. Whether the Quakers and their writing were both radical and popular is hard to judge, but there is no doubt of their broad and enduring significance.

NOTES

1. Christopher Hill, *The World Turned Upside Down. Radical Ideas during the English Revolution* (London; Temple Smith, 1972; Penguin; Harmondsworth, 1974 edition quoted); Hill, *Milton and the English Revolution* (London: Faber, 1977).

2. Hill, *World Turned Upside Down*, 231–2, 242–3.

3. Barry Reay, *The Quakers and the English Revolution* (London: Temple Smith, 1985), 1.

4. Christopher Haigh, *English Reformations. Religion, Politics and Society under the Tudors* (Oxford: Clarendon Press, 1993; 1994 edition quoted), 14–18, is the latest summing up of the "revisionist" position. For an eloquent discussion of the losses of the Reformation, see Eamon Duffy, *The Stripping of the Altars. Traditional Religion in England 1400–1580* (New Haven and London: Yale University Press, 1992).

5. John Morrill, "The Church in England," in John Morrill, ed., *Reactions to the English Civil War* (London; Macmillan, 1982).

6. *Radical Religion in the English Revolution*, ed. J.F. McGregor and B. Reay (Oxford; Clarendon Press, 1984).

7. Reay, *Quakers and the English Revolution*, 11, 44, makes brief mentions of the pamphlets but regards communication through print as only a minor part of the Quaker "story"; cf., B. Reay, "Quakerism and Society," in *Radical Religion*, ed. McGregor and Reay, 141–164.

8. J.C. Davis, *Fear, Myth and History. The Ranters and the Historians* (Cambridge; Cambridge University Press, 1986), see especially 42–3, for Davis's aims in looking at radicals' writings. Cf Davis's illuminating work on anti-formalism which nonetheless gathers together

material from a wide range of printed works whose precise context and purpose are not clarified: "Against Formality: One Aspect of the English Revolution," *Transactions of the Royal Historical Society* 6th series 3 (1993): 265–88. I am most grateful to Kate Peters for discussions on these issues.

9. David Underdown, *Revel, Riot and Rebellion. Popular Politics and Culture in England, 1603–1660* (Oxford: Oxford University Press, 1985), is a partial exception. His work clearly focuses on cultural divisions but he pays comparatively little attention to different uses of print culture or to prose writing specifically.

10. Tessa Watt, *Cheap Print and Popular Piety, 1550–1640* (Cambridge Studies in Early Modern British History), (Cambridge: Cambridge University Press, 1991).

11. Adam Fox, "Ballads, libels and popular ridicule in Jacobean England," *Past and Present* 145 (1994): 47–83.

12. For an example see Samuel Eaton, *The Quakers Confuted, being an Answer unto Nineteen Queries Propounded by them, and sent to the Elders of the Church of Duckenfield, Cheshire* (London, 1654).

13. Reay, *Quakers and the English Revolution*, 3.

14. Reay, *Quakers and the English Revolution*, 91–100.

15. Nigel Smith, *Perfection Proclaimed Language and Literature in English Radical Religion 1640–1660* (Oxford; Clarendon Press, 1989), and *Literature and Revolution in England, 1640–1660* (New Haven and London: Yale University Press, 1994).

16. Craig W. Horle, *The Quakers and the English Legal System, 1660–1688* (Philadelphia: University of Pennsylvania Press, 1988).

17. Alan Macfarlane, ed., *The Diary of Ralph Josselin 1616 –1683*, British Academy, Records of Social and Economic History, New Series 3, (Oxford, 1976): 366–7, diary entry for 11 April 1656.

18. Phyllis Mack, *Visionary Women. Ecstatic Prophecy in Seventeenth-Century England* (Berkeley, Los Angeles, Oxford: University of California Press, 1993).

19. Elaine Hobby, "Discourse so unsavoury: women's published writings of the 1650s," in Isobel Grundy and Susan Wiseman, eds., *Women, Writing, History 1640–1740* (London: Batsford, 1992), 16–32; Patricia Crawford, "Women's published writings 1600–1700," in Mary Prior, ed., *Women in English Society 1500-1800* (London: Methuen, 1985), 211–82, 213 for figures.

20. Mack, *Visionary Women*, 349.

21. Hill, *World Turned Upside Down*, 256–7, himself suggests some of the complexities.

22. Lyndal Roper, *Oedipus and the Devil: Witchcraft, sexuality and religion in early modern Europe* (London: Routledge, 1994), 155–57, for illuminating discussions of the incoherencies of reforming denunciations of the "world."

23. Christopher Hill, Barry Reay and William Lamont, *The World of the Muggletonians* (London: Temple Smith, 1983), 2–3.

Notes on Contributors

Norman T. Burns is Emeritus Associate Professor of English at the State University of New York at Binghamton. He wrote *Christian Mortalism from Tyndale to Milton* (Harvard University Press, 1972), and is currently studying Milton's commitment to an interior, spiritual religion.

Thomas N. Corns is Professor of English at the University of Wales, Bangor. He is author of *Uncloistered Virtue: English Political Literature, 1640–1660* (Clarendon, 1992) and *Regaining "Paradise Lost"* (Longman, 1994). With Ann Hughes and David Loewenstein, he is editing the works of Gerard Winstanley for Clarendon Press.

Judith Kegan Gardiner is Professor of English and Women's Studies at the University of Illinois at Chicago. She has published on Margaret Fell and Aphra Behn, and she edits the journal *Feminist Studies*.

Elaine Hobby is Reader in Women's Studies in the Department of English and Drama at the University of Loughborough. She is the author of *Virtue of Necessity: English Women's Writing, 1549–1688* (Virago, 1988). She is currently working on an edition of Jane Sharp, *The Midwives Book*, for Oxford University Press.

Ann Hughes is Professor of History at the University of Keele. She is the author of *The Causes of the English Civil War* (Macmillan, 1991), and is currently working on print culture and religious divisions in the 1640s and 1650s, and on a new edition of Winstanley.

N.H. Keeble is Reader in English at the University of Stirling. He is author of *Richard Baxter: Puritan Man of Letters* (Clarendon, 1982) and *The Literary Culture of Nonconformity in Later Seventeenth-century England* (Leicester University Press, 1987), and is working on the dissenter tradition across the early modern period.

John Knott is Professor of English at the University of Michigan. He is author of *The Sword of the Spirit: Puritan Responses to the Bible* (University of Chicago Press, 1980) and *Discourses of Martyrdom in English Literature, 1563–1694* (Cambridge University Press, 1993).

David Loewenstein is Professor of English at the University of Wisconsin-Madison. Heis the author of *Milton and the Drama of History: Historical Vision, Iconoclasm, and the Literary Imagination* (Cambridge University Press, 1990) and of *Milton: "Paradise Lost"* (Cambridge University Press, 1993). He is completing a study entitled *Representing Revolution in the Age of Milton and Winstanley*, and he is working on a new edition of Winstanley.

Kate Peters is completing a doctoral thesis on Quaker pamphletereering and the development of the Quaker movement to be submitted to the University of Cambridge. She is a lecturer in Modern History at the University of Birmingham.

Nigel Smith is Tutor and Fellow in English at Keble College, Oxford. He is the author of *Perfection Proclaimed: Language and Literature in English Radical Religion 1640–1660* and *Literature and Revolution in England, 1640–1660* (Yale University Press, 1994). He has recently edited Fox's *Journal* for Penguin, and is working on a new edition of Marvell.